Picture credits

Published by BBC Educational Publishing, BBC White City,
201 Wood Lane, London W12 7TS
First published 1999, Reprinted 1999 , Reprinted 2000
© Allan Todd/BBC Worldwide (Educational Publishing) 1999

ISBN: 0 563 46409 7

Printed by Bell & Bain Ltd, Glasgow

Schools History Project

Allan Todd

(Assistant Principal Examiner, GCSE History)

Contents

6

About BITESIZE History

BITESIZE History is a revision guide that has been specially put together to help you with your GCSE exams. You can tape the TV programmes and watch them on video, work your way through the activities and suggestions in this book, and even dial up the Internet on-line service.

It's called BITESIZE History because it's been divided up into manageable bitesize pieces of revision – much better than doing hours of revision the day before your exam! The video programmes, which give you information and advice, can be watched as often as you want until you have grasped all the points. Many video sections tie in with units in the book, which is divided into small sections that you can work through one by one. If you still don't understand something, you can contact the on-line team who are there to help you (see page 7 for website address).

How to use this book

This book is divided into three sections, sub-divided into units, which cover the three most popular GCSE topics of the Schools History Project syllabus. If you have any doubts about which topics you need to cover, ask your teacher.

Each unit of the book follows the same pattern:

- an introduction page which lists all the main areas you need to know about the topic. It also tells you what particular type of question you'll be practising, and the two mini-topics the questions will be based on

- a Factzone page, which gives more detailed historical information about the two mini-topics to be dealt with

- two pages of exam-type questions on those two mini-topics – one example question, with tips to help you understand what the examiner is looking for; and one practice question (also with reminders and hints to help you understand more clearly what the question is asking you to do).

For many of the units, there are corresponding sections on the video. In such cases, if you have videoed the programmes, it's a good idea to watch the video sequence(s) *after* reading the Factzone page, but *before* you try to work through or answer one of the questions. This is because the video sequences give you extra information and tips on how to answer exam questions. It's also a good idea to write the time codes from the video on the relevant page(s) of the book – this will help you find the video sequences quickly, as you go over units again.

KEY TO SYMBOLS

📺 A link to the video

⁇ Something to think about

◎ An activity to do

The most important sections of the GCSE Schools History Project syllabus (regardless of exam board) are covered by the book, but BITESIZE History doesn't aim to give total coverage of all topics. So it's important to carry on using your school textbook and your own notes. Since all the main types of GCSE

History questions are covered, the general tips and suggestions will be useful, even if some of your specific topics do not appear in the BITESIZE History book. Remember, the skills are transferable to the content of any topic.

The Schools History Project tries to get you to focus on key issues such as change and continuity, cause and consequence, and the factors associated with them. Medicine Through Time, in particular, covers a huge span of time. To help you focus on the key factors (e.g. war, chance) involved, the relevant ones for each period have been listed on the appropriate introduction pages.

The activities suggested in the book include:

- highlighting (either with highlighter pens, or by underlining or circling) certain bits in the sources and/or in the origin details which accompany the sources (i.e. the information about the sources provided by the Chief Examiner, such as date, country of origin, who wrote, produced or photographed it). This activity makes you look closely at the sources and the details of their origin. It's something you could usefully do on your final exam papers, to make sure you don't miss any points

- writing – either short-answer questions of one or two sentences, or more extended writing of several paragraphs or essays.

This book, on its own, will provide lots of useful revision practice. Taken together, the book and the video cover all the main skills required in GCSE History. NB If you are studying 'Germany' as your Depth Study, you will need to view 'Germany 1919–1945' from the Modern World History unit of programmes.

How to revise for GCSE History

There are three main aspects to successful revision, as opposed to unplanned, unfocused and therefore unsuccessful revision! These are:

- **organise:** prepare a long-term revision plan, in order to make the most of your time
- **learn:** make sure you know the relevant facts
- **apply:** understand and practise how to answer different types of questions.

Organise

You need to draw up a revision timetable to cover all your subjects – not just History! It should begin three or four months (not days!) before your exams start. Perhaps your school produces one – you could use that, or adapt it to suit your own needs. Once you've drawn up an outline timetable, divide the days (say, 90 or 100) by the number of subjects you're taking. This will tell you how many days you've got for revising History. Three very important things about revision are:

1 Don't try to revise for more than about 40 minutes at a time, otherwise you may overload your brain! About three 40-minute sessions per night is

THE ON-LINE SERVICE
You can find extra support, tips and answers to your exam queries on the BITESIZE Internet site. The address is http://www.bbc.co.uk/education/revision

enough for most people. Make sure your plan includes breaks (of at least 10–15 minutes) between each session. If you are revising hard, you'll need to take short breaks.

2 Be realistic – build in time off for activities like the cinema, sport or parties. One complete day off and one night off a week is reasonable. If you start early enough and you revise hard, you should be able to persuade your parents that some time off is okay!

3 Try to stick to your plan. If illness, for example, disrupts it, try to re-organise your plan to take account of this. Again, if you start early enough, you can get round problems like this without panicking.

Learn

This is much harder than drawing up a revision timetable. First of all, make sure that you know the exam requirements (such as topics, and the number and type of exam papers). If necessary, check with your teacher. Instead of rewriting your notes several times over, or simply re-reading your textbook, try some other revision methods:

- **highlight** or underline key terms and facts in your notes
- write these key points briefly on **index cards**
- draw **spider diagrams**
- listen to **tape recordings** of you (or a friend) reading out the main points
- ask someone to **test you** on a topic
- make **visual displays** of the main points of a unit on an A4 or A3 piece of paper, with brief facts in boxes, as in this example:

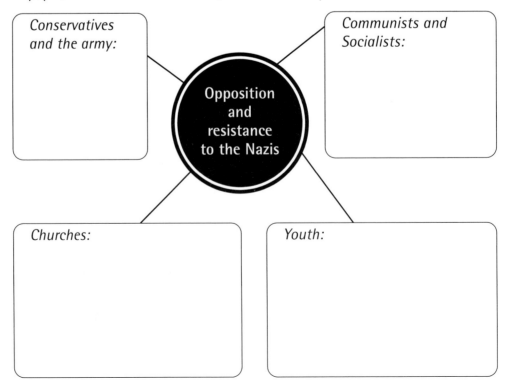

These diagrams can then be highlighted or underlined to help your memory. Put them up on your bedroom wall. You should be able to cover most topics in four or five pages at most.

Whatever methods you adopt, make sure you work in a quiet, warm room away from distractions. Try to keep your revision varied. For example, use a combination of note-making on cards, highlighting, writing fuller notes, and doing practice questions.

Apply

It's as important to practise answering the different types of questions as it is to learn the facts. For one History revision session, you could read through the Factzone on a topic, watch the video sequence (if there is one and you have recorded it), and then work through the example question. In your next revision session, you could read through the second part of the Factzone, watch any video sequence, and then do the practice question – making sure you follow the Remember points and the Think suggestions.

In particular, make sure that you look at, and work through, the full variety of questions, which range from:

■ **short-answer source comprehension/understanding and inference/recall questions** which simply ask you to pick out bits of information from a source and make inferences from your own knowledge about what the source does not show/explain

■ **short-answer comprehension in context questions** which require you to add facts from your own knowledge to the information given by a source

■ **source usefulness/source reliability questions** – both types require you to talk about a source and its provenance/origin details as regards:

1 nature/type: Is it primary or secondary? Was it written for a private or public audience? Is it a diary entry, or an official document?

2 author: Was it written/taken by someone in a position to know? Or is it likely to be biased? Or is it by someone (a historian, for example) who has done wide, and probably objective, research?

3 purpose: Was it written/taken in order to influence people (such as propaganda)? Or was it intended to be accurate (such as a report)?

4 typicality: Is the source representative/typical of people's thoughts on a particular situation? Or is it just a limited view of one person, time or place?

Remember, even a biased or unreliable source can be useful, for example, as evidence of how people thought, or as an example of propaganda. (Make sure you spell 'bias' and 'biased' correctly!)

■ **source comprehension/cross-referencing questions** which require you to pick out information from two or more sources and show how one source agrees and disagrees with another. The examiner is not trying to catch you out, so both sources will have differences as well as similarities.

- **change and/or continuity questions** which require you to analyse the extent of change (i.e. was it a turning point?) or continuity from one period to another. Alternatively, you may be asked to explain why change or continuity took, or did not take, place (i.e. by writing about the factors holding back or enabling change)

- **cause and consequence questions** which ask you to describe and explain the nature of a change and its consequences

- **analysis and judgement questions** which require you to think about the relative importance of some developments or individuals and to make a judgement (about which factor/individual was more/less important). Sometimes, you may be invited to agree/disagree with a statement made by the Chief Examiner.

- **extended writing questions**, either one or two paragraph questions, or essay questions, which require you to structure the facts you have revised into a logical, planned piece of writing. This is especially important for essays. For 'why' type essay questions, in particular, make sure you don't just write down everything you know. Instead, select and use only the facts relevant to the question. Always try to do a concluding/summary paragraph.

Finally, if some topics you're revising for the exam aren't in the book, or your particular topics are in the book but don't give you practice of all the types of questions above, don't panic. Look at the types of questions not covered, regardless of topic. The skills and tips are transferable to any topic.

On the day

Make sure you know which sections you have been prepared for. If in doubt, ask before the exam has started! Note carefully the total time available, and sort out the time you'll spend on each question, giving more time to those questions carrying the highest marks.

If there is a choice of questions, read through each one carefully, to ensure you choose the one(s) you know most about. For an essay question, make a rough plan first – it helps you find out right at the beginning whether you know enough about the topic (if you don't, it gives you time to select another!). It also gives you something to jot down in the last few minutes should you get into serious time trouble – you will get some marks for a note-style answer.

Finally, don't panic! If you have followed your teacher's advice and the suggestions in this book, you will be well-prepared for any question the Chief Examiner can think up. And remember, the exam is not meant to catch you out: it is designed to let you show what you know, understand and can do.

Now read on...

Good luck!

Revision notes

You can write notes here about the topics you have revised and those you still need to revise.

12

To be able to answer questions on this topic, you will need to know something about the following:

• finding out about prehistoric medicine – lack of evidence and problems in using what there is (cave paintings, bones showing survival after disease/injury, trephining/trepanning of skulls, no written evidence)

• evidence **by analogy** from more recent times (Australian Aborigines, Native Americans, Trobriand Islanders and medicine men)

• prehistoric theories – causes and cures (**supernatural**: evil spirits, magic and religion; **natural**: herbs and the treatment of cuts, broken bones, stomach disorders)

• importance of the development of writing in Ancient Egypt (recording of symptoms, treatments and success/failure; continuity and the development of medical knowledge)

FACTORS:
Religion
Practical methods
Communications

• Ancient Egyptian theories – causes and cures (**supernatural**: gods, goddesses, and evil spirits; connections between religious beliefs and treatment of illnesses; **natural**: herbal ointments and drugs, theory of **blockages**)

• religion, hygiene and surgery (priests and cleanliness; toilets and mosquito nets; embalming or 'mummification', and the study of anatomy; minor operations; the use of willow; surgical instruments)

• influence of Egyptian doctors and writings on the development of medicine in the ancient world (Sekhet' eanach, Imhotep; training: *Books of Thoth, Papyrus Ebers, Papyrus Edwin Smith, Papyrus Berlin*)

This section deals with prehistoric and Ancient Egyptian medicine, focusing on:

■ evidence from more recent times

■ Ancient Egyptian theories – causes and cures

This section gives you practice at answering comprehension and inference questions. Such questions require you to comprehend, and extract details from, the information provided by a source. They also require you to make some *inference* from the source(s), which must be linked to what is provided by the source(s).

FactZONE

You need to learn these key facts:

Evidence from more recent times

■ Since there is no *written* evidence about prehistoric medicine, historians have examined the medical beliefs and practices of various groups, which, in recent history, still lived like prehistoric people, i.e. nomadic hunter-gatherers living in small groups, with little or no contact with Europeans. By looking at such groups and their beliefs (e.g. late nineteenth century/early twentieth century Australian Aborigines, Native Americans, Trobriand Islanders), historians have tried to interpret prehistoric medical evidence (bones, trephined skulls).

■ Aborigines and Native Americans believed in spirits, consulted medicine men, and believed there were various causes for illnesses. Some medical problems, such as broken bones and cuts, had obvious **natural** causes, and were treated with commonsense, practical cures – rough mud and clay casts for broken bones; coverings of clay, herbs or animal skin or fat for cuts.

■ However, other health problems were not so straightforward – for these, **supernatural** explanations were given, e.g. evil spirits. People believed the evil spirits had to be driven out by magic and charms. Historians think such beliefs in the supernatural causes of diseases help explain why prehistoric skulls show clear evidence of trepanning operations, perhaps to drive out evil spirits. But, in the absence of written evidence of *prehistoric* beliefs, these can only remain theories.

Ancient Egyptian theories – causes and cures

■ Although the civilisation of Ancient Egypt was more advanced than that of prehistoric groups, there were some **similarities** of beliefs about illness. For example, the Ancient Egyptians believed in natural and supernatural causes and cures.

■ For illnesses with obvious **natural** causes, practical, common sense cures were used (e.g. willow bark as an antiseptic, use of herbal ointments and drugs, simple operations on cysts and tumours). As **writing** (on papyrus, a kind of paper made from reeds) had been invented, symptoms and cures were **recorded**. This allowed the **training** of later **doctors**, who had to follow strict rules and procedures.

■ However, even when natural cures were used, religious beliefs in Ancient Egypt (gods and goddesses causing and curing illnesses, evil spirits) meant doctors also used prayers and spells.

■ Most illnesses had no obvious causes – these were given **supernatural** explanations: *Sekhmet* was a goddess who caused and cured epidemics; *Thoth* was the god who gave doctors the skill to cure. To keep away evil spirits and illnesses sent by the gods, many people wore **charms** e.g. scarab beetle brooches, or amulets of the goddess *Taweret* (for safe pregnancy and childbirth).

■ The religious beliefs of Ancient Egyptians also helped the **development** of medical knowledge. For example, their belief in an after-life and the practice of embalming ('mummification') led to an increased knowledge of anatomy.

■ Egyptians' wide knowledge and expertise in irrigation systems led to the theory of **channels**. Illness was therefore caused by **blockages,** and cures included making patients vomit, or cutting veins to make them bleed.

Comprehension and inference questions

📺 Evidence from more recent times

Study sources A and B, which relate to evidence about medicine in prehistoric times, and then answer the question which follows.

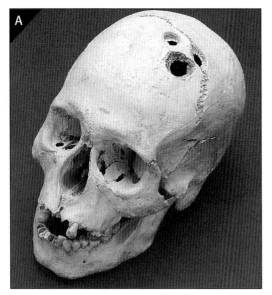

Source A A photograph of a prehistoric trephined skull.

Source B A drawing of a Native American medicine man, 1830.

 R E M E M B E R Comprehension and inference questions ask you to show that you understand the information in the source(s). You will need to extract two or three points from each source.

 R E M E M B E R To get high marks, you must do more than just describe what you can see in the source(s). Try to make some inference(s), based on what is in the source. Don't make assumptions which cannot be linked to the source(s).

◎ *What can you learn from Sources A and B about medicine in prehistoric times?*

Source A shows a large, smooth, round hole in the skull.

Inference: it is not a jagged hole, therefore it is not likely to have been caused by an accident. Its smooth, rounded edges mean that the person lived after the hole was cut. Therefore, prehistoric people were capable of performing surgery. But, there are no written records, so we cannot tell why it was done. However, it can be linked to beliefs and practices of more modern nomadic groups.

Source B shows a Native American medicine man but it doesn't show how he would attempt to cure a patient.

Inference: although not prehistoric, Native Americans had a similar way of life to prehistoric nomads. They used various methods to drive away evil spirits, so perhaps prehistoric medicine was based on similar beliefs and methods, but we can't be certain.

⚅ Ancient Egyptian theories: causes and cures

A

Here is the great remedy. Come! You who drive evil things from my stomach and my limbs. He who drinks this shall be cured just as the gods above were cured. This spell is really excellent – successful many times!

Look at the two sources here, which are both extracts from the *Papyrus Ebers*, dating from c.1500 BC.

Source A A spell to be chanted by the doctor while giving medicine to a patient.

B

46 vessels go from the heart to every limb. If a doctor, priest of Sekhmet, or magician, places his hand or fingers on the back of the head, hands, stomach, arms or feet, then he hears the heart. The heart speaks out of every limb. There are four vessels in his nostrils, two give mucus and two give blood.

There are four vessels to his two ears. The breath of life enters into the right ear, and the breath of death enters in the left ear...

When you come across a swelling that has attacked a vessel, then it has formed a tumour in his body. If, when you examine it with your fingers, it is like a hard stone, then you should say, 'It is a tumour of the vessels. I shall treat the disease with a knife'.

Source B An extract about vessels and tumours.

❓ *With the information you have gathered, try to make some general inferences or conclusions about medicine and its development in Ancient Egypt. Make sure any inferences are linked to specific aspects in the source(s).*

❓ *Consider what changes, if any, these sources suggest about the development of medicine since prehistoric times.*

❗ **REMEMBER** Look carefully at **both** sources and make sure you extract information from each one. Identify as many separate pieces of information as possible.

Practice question – Ancient Egyptian theories: causes and cures

Use the two sources above to answer the following question. Allow yourself 15 minutes.

■ What do sources A and B suggest about medicine in Ancient Egypt?

Greek and Roman medicine

To be able to answer questions on this topic, you will need to know something about the following:

• Ancient Greek beliefs – religious and rational (cult of **Asclepios**; attitudes to illness and death; influence of doctors of Ancient Egypt; rational theories and treatments)

• the importance of **Hippocrates** and his followers (search for natural explanations; clinical observation, diagnosis and treatment; lack of dissection and dangers of surgery; ethics and the Hippocratic Oath; medical books)

• later developments in Ancient Greece (Aristotle and the **Four Humours**; regimen/lifestyle to restore balance; importance of Alexandria for dissection, e.g. Herophilus and Erasistratus; library of medical books; legacy of Greek ideas)

• Roman attitudes to Greek medicine (conquest of Greek states, use of Greek doctors, continued belief in supernatural explanations for illnesses and cures)

FACTORS:
Religion
Scientific approach
Communications
Individuals
War

• practical observation and public health (draining of marshes; importance of clean water – aqueducts, tunnels and syphons; public baths and toilets)

• the significance of military factors (need for healthy soldiers; hospitals and treatment for the wounded)

• the importance of **Galen** (continued study of anatomy; writing of books; his legacy to medieval and Renaissance medicine)

This section deals with Ancient Greek and Roman medicine, focusing on:

■ later developments in Ancient Greece

■ the importance of Galen

This section will test your ability to answer continuity questions. These questions require you to extract information from the source(s) provided, *and* use your own knowledge, to show continuity in belief or practice from one period to another. Such questions often appear amongst the first few questions on the exam paper, and usually require only relatively short answers – perhaps only four or five sentences – so don't spend too long on them.

FactZONE

You need to learn these key facts:

Later developments in Ancient Greece

■ Building on the writings of Hippocrates (c. 460-377 BC) and his followers, who'd been mainly concerned with observation of the **symptoms** and **course** of illnesses, **Aristotle** (384-322 BC) developed their ideas into a theory about the **causes** and **treatments** of diseases:

■ **The Four Humours**: Aristotle suggested that the body was made up of four liquids, or humours – blood, phlegm, yellow bile, black bile. Any imbalance (e.g. colds and too much phlegm) was seen as a **cause**, not a **symptom**.

■ **Treatment** given by doctors was to 'restore the balance' between the humours: 'bleeding' to get rid of excess blood; vomiting if there was too much bile.

■ **Alexandria**, Egypt, was founded in 332 BC by Alexander the Great as the new capital of his huge empire. It contributed to the development of medicine in two ways:

■ its huge, famous **library** of important medical books
■ **dissection** was allowed (even of living criminals for a time), enabling progress in the study of **anatomy**.

■ **Legacy of Greek development**: though belief in supernatural causes and cures (Asclepios) continued, few new treatments were developed. While the theory of Four Humours (which lasted until the eighteenth century) was incorrect, Ancient Greece was important for:

■ advances in **anatomy**
■ the beginnings of a **scientific** approach to medicine (especially **clinical observation**)
■ doctors trained in Alexandria practised all over the Mediterranean world, spreading Greek ideas about how doctors should behave, the care of patients and the prevention of disease.

The importance of Galen

■ Born about AD 129, in Pergamum, Turkey, Galen trained as a doctor in the Asclepion there, and then in Alexandria. By then, for religious reasons, human dissection had been banned and he could only study skeletons. However, as a doctor to gladiators, he was able to study anatomy while treating wounds. When he moved to Rome, he took every opportunity to study bones (of criminals, or when cemeteries were flooded), as even the study of human skeletons was banned.

■ He followed Hippocrates' observation methods and believed in the theory of the four humours. He also developed many treatments, based on the theory of **opposites**, but he only wrote about his successes.

■ Deprived of human bodies, he dissected **animals** instead (barbary apes, pigs, dogs), so he made several mistakes (e.g. about the human brain and heart).

■ However, he was very important. He gave lectures and wrote over 100 books (many of which survived the fall of Rome), drawing together the ideas of all the great doctors of the ancient world in the 500 years since Hippocrates. He fitted everything into a single system, dealing with observation, diagnosis, treatments, surgery, anatomy and physiology.

■ As he used the term 'the creator' in his books, his theories were acceptable to Christians and Muslims. They formed the basis of doctors' training during the Middle Ages and the Renaissance.

Continuity questions

ⓣ Later developments in Ancient Greece

Study sources A and B, and use your own knowledge, to answer the question below.

Source A Extract from a history text book, published in 1996, about the beliefs of Ancient Egyptians.

> **A**
> Because the Egyptians left written records, we know what they thought caused illnesses and also how they treated them. The Egyptians believed that many diseases were caused by an evil spirit entering the body. They often wore charms to keep these spirits away. If they became ill despite the charms, they turned to magic and the gods to make them well.

> **B**
> Aegestratos was unable to sleep because of headaches. As soon as he came to the temple he fell asleep and had a dream. He thought that the god cured him of his headache and, making him stand up, taught him wrestling. The next day he departed cured, and after a short time he competed at the Nemean games and was victor in the wrestling.

Source B Inscription from a carved stone tablet found at a temple of Asclepios, long after the time of Hippocrates.

 REMEMBER This is a question about continuity, not about change, development, or differences. So make sure that this is what you focus on in your answer. Refer to both sources.

◎ *What continuity in beliefs about the causes and treatment of illnesses was there between Ancient Egypt and Ancient Greece?*

⁇ *Think of how you can use your own knowledge to add to what is provided by the two sources. If you don't deal with both parts of the question - sources and own knowledge - you will not be able to achieve the higher marks.*

Both **sources** show the belief that diseases had supernatural causes and cures (source A refers to charms, magic and the gods; source B refers to a temple and a god).

From your own knowledge, make specific reference to Ancient Egyptian gods (Sekhmet, Taweret, Thoth), and to the cult of Asclepios and the building of Asclepions (healing temples). You could also, briefly, mention that both societies also had common sense, natural theories and treatments, and that both developed knowledge of anatomy ('mummification' in Ancient Egypt, dissection at Alexandria).

◎ *Highlight any relevant points, provided by the sources and/or by the details of their origins.*

📺 The importance of Galen

Study sources A and B, and then answer the question below.

A Dissection was allowed in Alexandria – for a short time even dissection of the living was carried out. Criminals, who were condemned to die, were dissected and consequently the movement of blood around the veins was discovered. This practice was soon stopped. But dissection of the dead was still carried out, and advances in anatomy were made. The work carried out at Alexandria stressed accurate observation of what was actually there.

Source A An extract from a history textbook, published in 1996, about dissection in Alexandria.

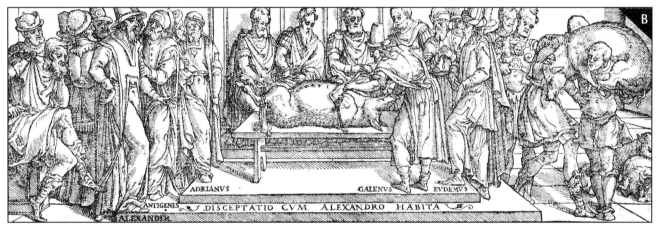

Source B Galen dissecting a pig. From a 1556 edition of Galen's *Collected Works*.

❓ *Think carefully about what you know about these periods and try to be precise and detailed in the information you provide (i.e. names, dates, etc.). Try to avoid broad, generalised comments.*

❗ R E M E M B E R Look carefully at both sources first, then extract any useful evidence (i.e. which shows continuity). Don't forget to look carefully at the information provided by the Chief Examiner.

Practice question – the importance of Galen

Use the sources, and your own knowledge, to write one or two paragraphs to answer the following question. Allow yourself 15 minutes.

■ What continuity was there in the development of medical knowledge between Ancient Greek and Ancient Roman times?

Islamic and medieval medicine

To be able to answer questions on this topic, you will need to know something about the following:

• the impact of the collapse of the Roman Empire (loss of Greek and Roman texts, survival of Byzantine or Eastern Empire, role of **Nestorius** and his followers)

• medicine and the Islamic Empire (**Hunain ibn Ishaq** [Johannitius] and the preservation of works by Hippocrates and Galen; development of Islamic medicine and hospitals; spread of Arabic ideas to Europe via trade and crusades)

• important individuals in Islamic medicine (**Rhazes** and his *al-Hawi*; **Ibn Sina** [Avicenna]; **Abul Kasim** [Albucasis] and surgery; attitude of the Islamic religion to dissection; developments in **anatomy** and **chemistry**)

• the role of the Christian Church in Western Europe (belief in supernatural causes and cures; pilgrimages, saints and prayers; control of medical ideas; attitude to Galen in the Middle Ages)

FACTORS:
Religion
Scientific approach
Communications
Individuals
War
Government

• medieval medical ideas and developments (importance of Hippocrates and Galen; physicians and surgeons; links with the Islamic world; establishment of medical schools and university departments; dissection; lack of significant changes; hospitals; comparisons with Islamic medical knowledge)

• public health – regression and continuity (towns; monasteries and hospitals; epidemics and plagues – beliefs about causes and cures; the Black Death)

This section deals with Islamic and medieval medicine, focusing on:

■ important individuals in Islamic medicine

■ medieval medical ideas and developments

This section gives you practice at answering analysis and judgement questions. Such questions require you to use your own knowledge to agree or disagree with a particular judgement of some historical period or event.

You need to examine arguments for *and* against the judgement given in the question. You will need to support your argument closely by providing appropriate and precisely selected knowledge.

FactZONE

You need to learn these key facts.

Important individuals in Islamic medicine

■ **Rhazes** (860-925): he followed the Hippocratic methods of **clinical observation**, and was the first to note the different symptoms of smallpox and measles. He wrote an important book: *al-Hawi* or *The Comprehensive Book.*

■ **Ibn Sina** (980-1037) aka **Avicenna**. His *Canon of Medicine* (a complete medical system, based on Galen and new observations) was later translated into Latin, becoming the main medical textbook in Europe until 1700.

■ **Abul Kasim** (936-1013) aka **Albucasis** – the greatest Arab surgeon – wrote a book on surgery, containing advice on amputations, fractures and dislocations, and dentistry. He was the first to write about haemophilia.

■ **Ibn an-Nafis** made many observations during operations (the Qur'an forbade dissection) and discovered **some errors in Galen** (in 1242, he said blood passed through the lungs). But no-one else agreed, so the old views continued.

■ Other important developments included:
hospitals: the Qur'an emphasised the duty to care for the sick and to study medicine. By 850, Baghdad had its first hospital.

chemistry: Islamic 'alchemists' made great advances e.g. **distillation** and **sublimation**. These methods were then used in preparing drugs. New drugs were developed (e.g. laudanum, camphor).

Medieval medical ideas and developments

■ Until about 1200, there was little organised study of medicine or training of doctors in Europe. Universities were controlled by the Church, which insisted that the Bible, Hippocrates and Galen explained everything.

■ However, increased contact with the Islamic world led to more knowledge of Hippocrates and Galen and to the establishment of **medical schools**. By the fourteenth century, medical departments were being set up in universities.

■ By about 1300, the Church began to allow some public dissection in universities and some revisions of Galen. New methods were put forward (e.g. analysis of urine), but acceptance of new ideas was very slow (e.g. early attempts at anaesthetics by surgeons such as **John of Arderne**).

Particularly important were:
■ **Hugh** (d. 1252) and **Theoderic of Lucca** (1205-98): used wine to clean wounds and reported its success (as an early antiseptic), but their idea did not catch on.

■ **Mondino de Luzzi** (c. 1270-1326) aka **Mundinus**: his *Anatomy* of 1316 became the main teaching text for the next 200 years.

■ **Guy de Chauliac** (c. 1300-68) wrote *Chirurgia Magna* in 1363 – the most important medieval book on surgery.

■ Despite these developments, medical knowledge in medieval Europe was often less advanced than that in the Islamic world.

Analysis and judgement questions

Important individuals in Islamic medicine

Look at the source below, which is an eighth-century drawing of Islamic doctors performing a Caesarean section operation. This was a technique known to doctors in Ancient Greece, India and Rome.

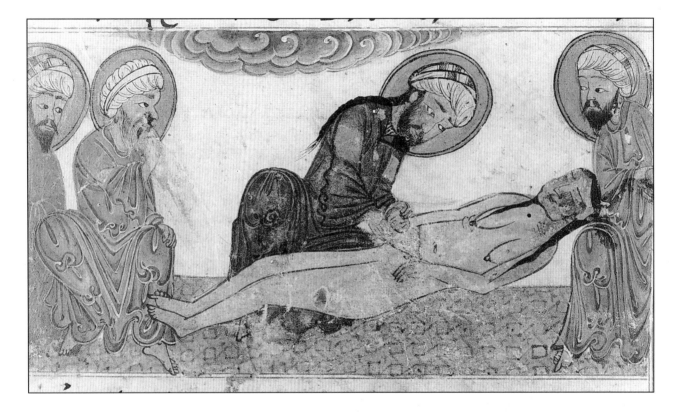

 'Medicine in the Arab world in the period AD 750-1400 was unable to advance because of Islamic religious beliefs'. Use the source above, and your own knowledge, to explain whether or not you agree with this statement.

REMEMBER Stick to the question, which is about Islamic and Arabic medicine. Don't write in detail about developments in Ancient Greece or Rome.

To answer questions like this, it is important to realise that the Chief Examiner does not expect you to simply agree with the statement. Such statements are always more complex, and are based on the fact that there are always other sides, or factors, to be considered.

For this question, as well as selecting appropriate knowledge to show how the Islamic religion both discouraged medical progress (e.g. dissection) and encouraged it (e.g. hospitals), you will need to write about how Arab doctors used and added to the ideas and work of people such as Galen. It would also be useful to point out how Islamic medicine was, in many ways, superior to that in medieval Europe.

📺 Medieval medical ideas and developments

Look at the source below, which is the title page of the 1493 edition of Mondino de Luzzi's *Anatomy*, written in 1316. It shows Mondino reading from a book while an assistant dissects a body.

❓ *Think about how you can give a balanced answer to the practice question below. For instance, you could point out how the Christian Church's attitude to dissection changed, as well as giving evidence of the Church's attitude to illnesses and their causes and cures, and the emphasis on sticking to what was known of Galen's writings.*

❗ R E M E M B E R
Don't simply agree with the statement. It has been deliberately phrased to encourage you to look for ways in which to disagree with the statement, or at least add to it.

Practice question – medieval medical ideas and developments

Write three or four paragraphs to answer the following question, making reference to the source above. Allow yourself 20 minutes.

■ 'The Christian religion dominated medical thinking and prevented any progress in Europe throughout the Middle Ages'.

Do you agree or disagree? Explain your answer.

24

To be able to answer questions on this topic, you will need to know something about the following:

• impact of the Renaissance and Reformation (Church control of universities weakened; more accurate drawing/sculpture of human body, e.g. Michelangelo, **da Vinci**; development of printing; more scientific approach)

• rediscovery of Ancient Greek medical texts (rejection of Galen and Avicenna by **Paracelsus**; new translation of Galen's original and complete *On Anatomical Procedures*, 1531; corrections to Mondino de Luzzi's work; more scientific anatomy)

• sixteenth-century developments in anatomy and treatment (**Vesalius**, 1514-64; discovery of errors in Galen's anatomy of the heart; *The Fabric of the Human Body*, 1543; work of **Colombo**; impact on treatment)

• seventeenth-century developments in physiology (the influence of **Fabricius**; early work on the heart by **Harvey**, 1578-1657; *On the Motion of the Heart and Blood*, 1628; Sydenham, 1624-89, and *Medical Observations*, 1676; impact on treatment)

FACTORS:
Religion
Communications
Science and
technology
Individuals
War
Chance

• developments in surgery and treatment (significance of the Italian Wars; work of **Paré**, 1510-90; *Method of Treating Wounds*, 1545; surgery in Britain; reasons for lack of further progress)

• other development (**William and John Hunter** and improved training; hospital care; reduced role of women in medical care; continuation of alternative treatments).

This section deals with Renaissance medicine, c.1500-1750, focusing on:

■ sixteenth-century developments in anatomy and treatment

■ developments in surgery and treatment

This section tests your ability to answer change and continuity questions. These require you to analyse the key factors involved in promoting change and/or inhibiting change, and so leading to continuity. To get the higher marks, you will need to carefully select knowledge to illustrate the change(s), and to identify those factors which prevented wider acceptance/use.

FactZONE

You need to learn these key facts:

Sixteenth-century developments in anatomy and treatment

■ In 1531, **Guinter**, at the University of Paris, brought out a new translation of Galen's complete *On Anatomical Procedures*. This was a significant improvement on Mondino de Luzzi's *Anatomy* of 1316.

■ **Vesalius** (1514-64) did his own dissections, and published drawings of his work, e.g. *Tabulae Sex* in 1538, to help his students. But many doctors were opposed to this.

■ Vesalius found errors in Galen's anatomical work, but at first did not reject Galen's teachings publicly. In 1539, his *Letter on Venesection* criticised the current method of bleeding, based on his work on **veins**. This conflicted with the Arabic translations which had been followed since the Middle Ages and was rejected by many doctors.

■ In 1543, his seven-volumed *The Fabric of the Human Body* was published, with illustrations. In particular, he rejected Galen's theory that blood passed from one side of the heart to the other via the septum (already suggested by Ibn an-Nafis in 1242).

■ The Church and many doctors refused to accept Galen had made any errors. Vesalius took little part in the arguments and did not really carry his research further.

■ Vesalius did not offer any new theories about the **causes** of diseases or cures so his findings had little impact on the **treatment** of illness. Throughout the sixteenth century, treatment remained based on Hippocrates, the Four Humours, and Galen - with a wide range of **alternatives to physicians** for the majority of the population, e.g. apothecaries, barber-surgeons, 'quacks' or local 'wise women', who used bleeding, herbal remedies, astrology etc.

Developments in surgery and treatment

■ At first, most developments in surgery took place on the continent. Later, surgeons in **Edinburgh** and **London** made advances.

■ The most important Renaissance surgeon was **Paré** (1510-90). Initially trained as a barber-surgeon, he gained much experience as an army surgeon during the Italian Wars and the French Wars of Religion. He stressed the importance of first-hand **observation** over theory/books.

■ One important discovery came when he ran out of hot oil, traditionally used to **cauterise** (seal) **gunshot wounds**. He made a mixture of turpentine, rose oil and egg yolk instead and found this worked better. In 1545, he published his first book, *Method of Treating Wounds*.

■ Paré also used new ways of carrying out **amputations**. He used **ligatures** to stop excessive bleeding, and sealed blood vessels with **double silk thread** instead of using a 'cautery' (red-hot iron).

■ Paré continued to publish books about his new treatments (e.g. *Works on Surgery* in 1575) but most physicians stuck to the traditional methods.

■ However, since there were no **antiseptics**, Paré's use of thread meant wounds were more likely to go septic and kill the patient. In addition, the lack of **anaesthetics** meant surgery had to be quick and simple.

⊕ Sixteenth-century developments in anatomy and treatment

Study the sources A and B, which relate to Vesalius' advances in the knowledge of human anatomy.

Source A The title page of Vesalius' *The Fabric of the Human Body* of 1543, showing him carrying out an outdoors dissection, with a crowd of observers.

The jaws of most animals is formed of two bones joined together at the apex of the chin. In man, however, the lower jaw is formed of a single bone. Nevertheless Galen and most of the skilled dissectors since the time of Hippocrates stated that the jaw is not a single bone. In spite of this, so far no human jaw has come to my attention constructed of two bones.

Source B An extract from *The Fabric of the Human Body*, showing Vesalius' questioning of Galenic anatomy.

◎ *Use the sources above, and your own knowledge, to explain why Vesalius' discoveries did little to improve medical treatment.*

❗ REMEMBER When answering questions like this, be sure you give **explanations**, not a description of what Vesalius did. The question asks you to use the sources, as well as your own knowledge. Make sure you refer to **both** sources.

Questions like this require you to examine the nature of change and factors that stopped the change being followed up, i.e. which contributed to the maintenance of tradition and continuity.

Source A shows that Vesalius carried out dissections himself, therefore he must have been able to make detailed observations.
Source B shows that Vesalius' scientific methods led him to notice errors in Galen, based on observation.

From your own knowledge, consider that although Vesalius provided the first really accurate description of human anatomy, many refused to accept his findings as they contradicted Galen, whose work had been followed for centuries. Also, Vesalius did not really comment on the causes and cures of illnesses. Other advances were needed before his anatomical discoveries could be linked to treatment.

Developments in surgery and treatment

Look at the sources below, which relate to Paré's contributions to surgery.

A

After a time I ran out of oil, and I had to apply instead a digestive made of yolks of egg, oil of roses and turpentine. That night I could not sleep at my ease, fearing that because I had not cauterised them I should find the wounded dead or poisoned. This made me get up very early to visit them.

Beyond my hope I found those on whom I had put the digestive medicament feeling little pain, and their wounds without inflamation, having rested fairly well throughout the night. The others to whom I had applied the boiling oil, I found feverish, with great pain and swelling about their wounds. Then I resolved with myself never more to burn thus cruelly poor men wounded with gunshot.

Source A An extract from Paré's *Apology and Treatise* of 1585 explaining how he discovered a new method of treating gunshot wounds.

B

When you have cut off the limb, let it bleed a little so that the rest of the part may afterwards be less likely to become inflamed. Then let the veins and arteries be tied up as speedily as you can so that the flowing of the blood may be stopped. The ends of the vessels lying hidden in the flesh must be drawn out with this instrument [crow's beak]. When you have so drawn them forth, bind them with double thread.

Source B An extract from Paré's *Works on Surgery* of 1575 outlining his new method of how to stop bleeding after amputations.

(?) *Think carefully about the practice question below. As well as using your own knowledge to briefly explain what Paré's discoveries were, make sure you explain the various factors which prevented his ideas from leading to any immediate and widespread improvement in surgery.*

Practice question – developments in surgery and treatment

Use the sources above, and your own knowledge, to write three or four paragraphs to answer the following question. Allow yourself 25 minutes.

■ Explain why Paré's discoveries did not immediately lead to any major breakthrough or progress in surgery during the Renaissance period.

28

To be able to answer questions on this topic, you will need to know something about the following:

• the state of medicine by 1750 (impact of seventeenth-century Scientific Revolution; **van Leeuwenhoek** and the microscope, 1683; greater respect for physicians and doctors; improved training and standards; persistence of old ideas; 'quackery')

• the impact of the Industrial Revolution (increased confidence in science and progress; improved technological aids for medicine; effects on public health of towns and population)

• the significance of **Jenner's** work (Jenner's scientific training; **inoculation**; early observations; **vaccination** experiment; reactions and impact)

FACTORS:
Religion
Science and technology
Communications
Individuals
War
Government
Chance

• **germ theory** and infectious diseases ('miasmas' and 'spontaneous generation' theories; microscopes and **germs**; **Pasteur's** early discoveries; **Koch's** work on human diseases, building on Pasteur's work; improved communications)

• **anti-toxins** and curing disease (later developments by Pasteur and Koch – rivals because of the Franco-Prussian War 1870-71; **Behring's** discovery of anti-toxins; the **cure** for diphtheria, 1891)

This section deals with industrialisation and nineteenth-century medicine, focusing on:
■ the significance of Jenner's work
■ anti-toxins, and curing disease

This section tests your ability to answer causation questions. Such questions require you to use your own knowledge to describe and analyse the various key features or factors which led to a particular change or development. It is important to look for more than one factor – there is invariably a *range* of factors involved in any significant change. Sometimes, some reasons can be identified as being more important than others.

FactZONE

You need to learn these key facts:

The significance of Jenner's work

■ Doctors in the eighteenth century were better trained in anatomy, chemistry and observation. **Jenner**, who had studied under John Hunter, was one doctor who observed his patients more closely.

■ **Smallpox** had become a common disease. An early method used to fight it was **inoculation** (used in China and Turkey, and brought to England in 1718 by Lady Mary Wortley Montagu). This involved infecting people with a mild form of the disease in the hope they would not catch the serious version. However, some of these people still died.

■ **Edward Jenner** (a country doctor in Gloucestershire) heard the local belief that milkmaids who caught the milder disease of cowpox never caught smallpox. After years of observation, he experimented on **James Phipps** in 1796, infecting him with pus from the sores of **Sarah Nelmes** (a milkmaid suffering from cowpox). When Phipps had recovered, he then gave him a dose of smallpox. The boy did not develop the disease, so he then infected 23 others and it still worked.

■ Jenner called his method **vaccination** and published his results in 1798. He met much opposition. He was an unknown country doctor, and was unable to explain why his method worked. An Anti-Vaccine Society was even set up.

■ But many supported his methods (including the royal family and Napoleon). He received money from Parliament, which made vaccination free for all infants in 1840. Vaccination was made compulsory in 1853. This was very unusual as, at this time, governments were reluctant to intervene in such matters (though in parts of Germany vaccination had been compulsory since 1807).

■ While it was another eighty years before another vaccine was discovered, Jenner had begun the attempt to combat disease by **immunisation**.

Anti-toxins and curing disease

■ Jenner had discovered how to prevent a disease (by **vaccination**); **Pasteur** (helped by more powerful microscopes) had discovered how **germs** caused diseases in plants and animals. **Koch** had discovered how microbes caused wounds to go septic (1878) and later identified germs causing diseases in **humans** e.g. TB (1882) and cholera (1883).

■ But still there was no **cure** for those already infected with a disease. The important breakthrough here was made by **Emil von Behring**, one of Koch's assistants. He took a discovery made by Pasteur's team (that germs caused diseases by producing **toxins** [poisons] in the blood stream), and found that some animals produced an **anti-toxin** to fight the poison.

■ Behring experimented by extracting the anti-toxins and injecting them into **humans**. These destroyed the poisons caused by the germs.

■ The first **cure** of an ill human, by the use of an anti-toxin, was in 1891 (of a child with diphtheria). Soon, other anti-toxins were developed.

Causation questions

📺 The significance of Jenner's work

Study the two sources below, which refer to Jenner's discovery of the smallpox vaccine.

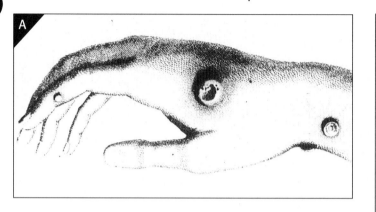

Source A Jenner's drawing of the cowpox lesion he used to develop his vaccine.

Source B Jenner's account of his vaccination experiment, published in 1798.

> I selected a healthy boy about eight years old for the purpose of inoculation with the smallpox. The matter was taken from a suppurated sore on the hand of a dairy Maid who was infected by her master's Cows, and it was inserted on the 14th of May 1796, into the arms of the Boy, by means of two superficial incisions, each about three quarters of an inch long... On the 1st of July following, this Boy was inoculated with Matter immediately taken from a smallpox Pustule. Several punctures and slight incisions were made in both his arms, and the matter was well rubb'd into them, but no disease follow'd.

◎ *What factors made Jenner's development of vaccination possible by the end of the eighteenth century?*

⁉ *Think carefully how you can use your own knowledge to show what had happened before 1796 to make Jenner's discovery possible. Try to identify two or more factors and consider how you can clearly demonstrate their significance.*

❗ **REMEMBER**
This is a causation question, so you need to do much more than just **describe** what Jenner did.

The main factors were:

■ impact of the seventeenth-century Scientific Revolution

■ improved training of doctors in the eighteenth century (including stress on clinical observation)

■ the method of inoculation, which paved the way for Jenner

■ chance: without knowing the cause of the disease, Jenner (by observation and luck) discovered that a relatively harmless human disease gave cross-immunity to a more serious one.

📺 Anti-toxins and curing disease

Look at the two sources below, which relate to Behring's discovery of anti-toxins.

Source A Members of Pasteur's team removing saliva from a rabid dog, in order to develop a vaccine for rabies.

Vaccination is a method of preventing disease. It was Koch's assistant, Emil Behring, who produced the first actual cure based on the germ theory. Pasteur's team had discovered that germs cause disease by producing poisons, or 'toxins', in the blood-stream. Behring then found that some animals produced an 'anti-toxin' in their blood to fight the poison.

This substance could be extracted and injected into humans where it, in turn, would destroy the poisons caused by the germs. On Christmas Day 1891, a child was cured of diphtheria (a bacterial infection which blocks the throat) by the first use of the anti-toxin.

Source B Extract from a history textbook, published in 1996.

❓ *Think carefully about what had happened in medicine earlier in the nineteenth century that can be linked to Behring's work.*

◎ *Look carefully at your textbook and your notes before answering the practice question below.*

❗ REMEMBER
The practice question requires you to give a variety of reasons to explain **why** something happened when it did. Jot down a rough list of factors first, then focus on explaining **how** these helped Behring make his discovery.

Practice question – anti-toxins and curing disease

Write four or five paragraphs to answer the question, making reference to the sources above. Allow yourself 25 minutes.

■ Why was Behring able to make his breakthrough cure of diphtheria in 1891?

To be able to answer questions on this topic, you will need to know something about the following:

• **Ehrlich** and 'magic bullets' (his early work with Behring; discovery by Koch and his teams how some chemical dyes, used to stain microbes to aid examination under the microscope, killed the microbes; antibodies and 'magic bullets'; **Hata** and Salvarsan 606; reactions)

• **Domagk** and sulphonamides

• the work of **Fleming** (early work with Wright; work in a military hospital in the First World War; research into septic wounds; chance discovery of **penicillin**, 1928; failure to purify the 'mould juice')

• later developments 1938-42 (Howard **Florey** and Ernst **Chain**; experiments in 1940 with pure penicillin; production problems)

• the final stages (the Second World War; the US chemical industry; mass production of penicillin; later developments)

FACTORS:
Science and technology
Communications
Individuals
War
Government
Industry
Finance
Chance

This section deals with the Drugs Revolution 1900-50, focusing on:

■ Ehrlich and 'magic bullets'

■ the work of Fleming

This section gives you practice at answering evaluation of change questions. Such questions require you to analyse or assess the nature of a change or development, and the extent to which it did/did not bring about significant change.

Such questions frequently ask you to decide whether or not a particular discovery or development was a turning point in the history of medicine. To do this, you need to use your own knowledge to show what the situation was like *before* and *after* the discovery, and then to assess whether it led to revolutionary changes.

FactZONE

You need to learn these key facts:

Ehrlich and 'magic bullets'

■ In 1899, as head of his own research institute, **Paul Ehrlich** became interested in **antibodies**. These were produced naturally by the body to fight specific germs without harming the rest of the body. Ehrlich called these antibodies 'magic bullets', but antibodies did not always work. So he and his team began to look for synthetic **chemical** 'magic bullets' to cure disease. At first, Ehrlich had only limited success (though dyes were found that attacked malaria and sleeping sickness germs). In 1906, Schaudinn and Hoffman identified the **syphilis** microbe and in the following year, Ehrlich began to search for a chemical 'magic bullet' for this disease.

■ In 1909, after his team had tested over 600 dyes, **Sahachiro Hata** joined the team. He retested the dyes, and found that dye 606 worked – this became known as **Salvarsan 606**. After testing it on hundreds of animals deliberately infected with syphilis, it was first tried on a human in 1911.

■ However, there was much opposition (it was difficult and painful to inject, while some feared it would encourage promiscuity). It was over twenty years before a second 'magic bullet' was discovered (by Domagk in 1932).

The work of Fleming

■ In 1906, **Alexander Fleming** began work as a research assistant under Sir Almroth Wright (who had discovered a vaccine against typhoid in 1896). During the First World War, his work in a military hospital (where antiseptics were used, not very successfully, to prevent infections in wounds) led him to seek a more effective way of killing germs. In 1922, he discovered that **lysozyme** (found in tears) killed some germs, but not those causing disease and infection.

■ In 1928, he began work on **staphylococci** (germs that make wounds septic). One day, by chance, Fleming noticed mould was growing on the agar of some Petri dishes waiting to be cleaned. But, more importantly, he noticed that no germs were growing near the mould. Though he had no idea how the mould had entered his laboratory, Fleming then grew it, tested it on various deadly germs, and found it killed almost all of them.

■ A colleague identified the mould as one of the penicillium family (first noticed by Lister in 1871). Although at first he tried to purify the 'mould juice', the necessary chemical skills were unavailable. After he had tested it on animals, and showed it did no harm, he tried it on a colleague's eye infection. Again, it worked, and did no harm to body tissues. In 1929 and 1931, he wrote up his research and findings in the *British Journal of Experimental Pathology*. He called the 'mould juice' **penicillin**.

■ Though this drug (the first derived from a living organism) seemed much better than the sulphonamide drugs, as it worked on almost all the serious microbes and yet caused no damage to the body, Fleming did not persist in trying to make pure penicillin.

■ Instead of carrying out the huge amount of research necessary, Fleming returned to his more routine work (on bacteria and vaccines). Work by others would be necessary to develop this first **antibiotic** properly.

Evaluation of change questions

⊡ Ehrlich and 'magic bullets'

Study the source below about the discovery of a cure for syphilis. The extract describes part of the research into the effectiveness of dye 606.

> Ehrlich looked at the records and said, 'No, surely not! It was all minutely tested by Dr R. and he found nothing. More than a year ago we laid aside 606 as worthless. You are sure that you are not mistaken, Dr Hata?
>
> Hata pointed to the records of the experiments, and said, 'I found that, Herr Direktor'.
>
> 'Then it must be repeated, dear Hata,' said Ehrlich.
>
> The treatment with 606 had amazingly successful results, but Ehrlich demanded that it should be repeated over and over again with hundreds of experimentally infected animals. At length Ehrlich convinced himself of the outstanding curative power of 606.

◎ *To what extent was Ehrlich's discovery of Salvarsan 606 in 1909 a turning point in the history of medicine?*

⑦ *Consider carefully what is meant by the concept 'turning point', and see how you can use your own knowledge to assess or evaluate the discovery. Try to consider arguments for and against, before you make your conclusion.*

❗ REMEMBER
Jot down some points in rough before you begin to write your answer. The examiner who marks your answer will be much more impressed by a clearly-ordered argument.

For: Salvarsan was the first man-made chemical 'magic bullet' which could be used to kill microbes and so cure a disease. Before then, methods used were **vaccinations** (Jenner) or **anti-toxins** taken from animals (**Behring**).

Though it was over twenty years before another 'magic bullet' was discovered, it pointed the way forward – others (**sulphonamides**) were discovered in 1932 and 1935; and it could be said to have led to the discovery of **penicillin**.

Against: many doctors were reluctant to use it (injections were painful; they didn't like using arsenic in any form; it might encourage promiscuity as it cured syphilis). Also, a second 'magic bullet' was not discovered until 1932.

📺 The work of Fleming

Study the source below, which refers to Fleming's discovery of the effects of penicillin.

Extract from Fleming's article of 1929 in the *British Journal of Experimental Pathology*.

> **It is suggested that penicillin may be an efficient antiseptic for application to, or injection into, areas infected with penicillin-sensitive microbes.**

This type of practice question requires you to assess the significance of particular changes, developments or discoveries. To do this, you will need to:

■ analyse the extent to which it marked a real advance on the knowledge and/or treatment that existed **before** the discovery

■ discuss the extent to which it changed future knowledge and/or treatment.

🤔 *Try to think about the state of medicine before and after Fleming made his discovery, and try to use precise factual details.*

◎ *Jot down your rough points without looking at the Factzone.
Then look carefully at your textbook and your notes.*

◎ *Now watch the video sequence on Fleming, if you have recorded it, before writing your final version.*

Practice question – the work of Fleming

Write four or five paragraphs to answer the following question. Allow yourself 20 minutes.

■ How far was Fleming's discovery of pencillin in 1928 a turning point in the history of medicine?

To be able to answer questions on this topic, you will need to know something about the following:

• rapid change and 'high tech' medicine (increased vaccination; greater variety of drugs; improvements in surgery; improvements in nursing; specialist hospitals; war and increased government funding)

• problems with some methods and drugs (problems of 'high-tech' surgery; side-effects of some drugs, e.g. Thalidomide, tranquillisers etc; resistance to antibiotics)

• new health problems and diseases (modern lifestyles e.g. smoking, poor diet, lack of exercise; pollution and allergies; ageing population; NHS costs; new diseases, e.g. AIDS, CJD)

FACTORS:
Science and technology
Communications
Government
Industry
Finance
Social attitudes
Chance

• changing attitudes to public health (impact of war; increased democracy and communications; setting up of the NHS; housing; waste disposal)

• the Third World (epidemics, famine and population control; UN, WHO and 'Health for all by 2000')

• alternative and non-European medicine (acupuncture, homeopathy, chiropractic and herbal medicine; medicine in Asia, Africa and Latin America)

This section deals with medicine now 1950-2000, focusing on:

■ problems with some methods and drugs

■ alternative and non-European medicine

This section gives you practice at answering comprehension and cross-referencing questions. Such questions require you to show that you can:

(i) understand the information provided by two (or more) sources

(ii) demonstrate the extent to which the sources support and do *not* support each other on a particular issue.

Very often, in order to obtain the higher marks, you will need to make some inferences about the information provided by the sources and give a *brief* indication of what further evidence would have been useful.

FactZONE

You need to learn these key facts:

Problems with some methods and drugs

■ Despite the tremendous advances made since 1900, various problems still exist in twentieth-century medicine.

■ 'High-tech' surgery is highly successful. It can carry out complicated operations with low risk to the patient. However, there are some problems. Complex surgery means mistakes can be serious; there are moral or ethical problems (e.g. transplants, use of life-support machinery); modern surgery is also very expensive – how much is society prepared to pay?

■ There have been problems with modern medicines – large companies can make huge profits by selling drugs: sometimes, new drugs are marketed without being fully tested. Some side-effects have been disastrous, e.g. Thalidomide, Largactil.

■ Some vaccinations have also been associated with side-effects, e.g. epilepsy, brain damage. Some diseases are increasing again, as parents' fears are leading to reductions in the number of children vaccinated.

■ In addition, many viruses and germs have become resistant to some antibiotics (including penicillin) and mutate more quickly than new antibiotics can be developed. So not all infectious diseases have been fully conquered (some hope genetic engineering and biochemistry will provide the answers).

Alternative and non-European medicine

■ 'High-tech' medicine in the twentieth century has not meant traditional or alternative medicine has disappeared - not only in Asia, Africa and Latin America, but also in Europe and North America.

■ Traditional methods in Europe include herbal medicine (often using herbalist recipes from the Middle Ages), 'nature cures' (based on diet and exercise, similar to the Ancient Greek idea of 'regimen'), acupuncture (using a theory of physiology used by the Chinese for centuries) and visits to 'faith' or spiritual healers of various kinds.

■ Problems with 'high-tech' medicine have led many to turn to traditional or alternative medicine – numbers have increased dramatically since the 1980s (in 1981, a survey showed that about 10 million people in Britain had consulted an 'alternative practitioner').

■ Many of these 'alternative practitioners' (e.g. chiropractors, osteopaths, psychotherapists, acupuncturists, hypnotherapists) are organised in their own professional bodies, and several thousand qualified doctors occasionally practice such methods alongside modern methods. Some alternative treatments are available under the NHS in some regions. Generally, however, the British Medical Association remains doubtful about the usefulness of such methods.

Comprehension and cross-referencing

Problems with some methods and drugs

Study the two sources below, which refer to problems associated with some modern drug treatments.

A

More than 9000 new drugs (have been developed) in the last 25 years. These drugs present new hazards as well as greater benefits than ever before for they are widely used, they are often very potent and they are presented by aggressive sales campaigns that may tend to overstate their merits and fail to indicate the risks involved in their use.

Source A President Kennedy's request for laws to control the sale of medical drugs, in his message to the US Congress in 1962.

Source B An extract from a school textbook on medicine, published in 1996.

B

Since the 1940s a number of unknown lethal diseases have developed. AIDS is the best known of these. Others include Lassa fever, Ebola virus, Dengue, Kuru, Machupo and Creutzfeld-Jacob disease.

One reason these diseases can spread rapidly is the ease of travel and communication today. Another reason is that viruses and germs have become resistant to some antibiotics and sometimes mutate more quickly than new antibiotics can be found to combat them.

 REMEMBER To get high marks, you must make **detailed** references to **all** the sources mentioned.

◎ *To what extent do sources A and B agree that modern medical drugs are the major cause of new health problems in the twentieth century?*

⁇ *Think carefully about what each source says and doesn't say. Try to show **how** they both agree **and** disagree with the question's statement.*

Similarities: Both sources refer to potential problems with drugs. Source A refers to 'new hazards' and 'risks', while Source B mentions how some viruses/germs are now 'resistant to some antibiotics'.

Differences: Source A also refers to 'greater benefits' while Source B mentions new diseases (e.g. AIDS) and other factors (e.g. 'ease of travel and communication') as being the causes of new health problems.

◎ *Now highlight any points given in the sources and/or details of their origins, using one colour for similarities and another for differences.*

Alternative and non-European medicine

Study sources A and B below, which relate to the use of alternative medicine.

A

In one experiment, 62 patients with stomach ulcers were observed and evaluated by doctors trained in Western methods, but treated by traditional Chinese methods.

53 (81.5%) recovered
7 (10.8%) showed some improvement
2 (3.1%) showed no change

B

Types of alternative therapy personally experienced	Tried by	Satisfied? Yes %	No %
Herbal medicine	12	73	18
Osteopathy	67	31	4
Massage	6	82	9
Homeopathy	4	66	16
Acupuncture	3	50	47
Chiropractic	2	68	19
Hypnotherapy	2	43	50
Psychotherapy	2	75	12

Source A An extract from a book about Chinese medicine, published in 1983, about an experiment carried out in 1959.

Source B An extract from a survey on the popularity of alternative medicine, based on 2000 participants.

(?) *Think about how you can show how and where the two sources support and don't support the statement in the practice question below.*

◎ *Use two different colours to highlight any similarities and differences between the sources and/or the details of their origins.*

! **R E M E M B E R** Your references to **both** sources don't have to be long – just a brief quotation or a reference to specific lines.

Practice question - alternative and non-European medicine

Study sources A and B above, and write one or two paragraphs to answer the question. Allow yourself 15 minutes.

■ How far do sources A and B show that alternative medicine is as effective as modern 'high-tech' Western medicine?

Women and medicine

To be able to answer questions on this topic, you will need to know something about the following:

- the involvement of women before the Middle Ages (lack of trained doctors; reliance of ordinary people on family or local healers; women in all areas of medicine as physicians, surgeons, midwives, 'wise women', herbalists, healers and nurses, e.g. Fabiola in the fourth century)

- change and continuity in the Middle Ages (Church control of education; medical training becoming more professional; women edged out of medicine; trial of Jacoba, 1322; midwifery; medicine for ordinary people)

FACTORS:
Religion
Communications
Individuals
War
Government
Social attitudes
Education

- the impact of the Renaissance and the Scientific Revolution (greater knowledge of anatomy; more formal medical training; exclusion of women from universities; continuation of 'housewife-physicians' and local 'wise women')

- developments after 1750 (forceps and impact on midwives; the Crimean War and Florence Nightingale; the Nightingale School of Nursing and changes in nursing; attempts by women to qualify as doctors in the 1870s; opening of all medical qualifications to women in 1876 due to publicity, protests, changing attitudes to women and a growing shortage of doctors; medicine for the poorer classes)

- changes since 1900 (impact of First and Second World Wars; changing social attitudes; development of NHS; Dr. Mildred Berstock and typhus; greater equality).

This section deals with women and medicine, focusing on:

- change and continuity in the Middle Ages

- developments after 1750

This section gives you practice at answering utility questions. These require you to evaluate sources for their usefulness in aiding understanding of a particular situation or development. To get higher marks, you must deal with what information the source(s) provide *and* comment (if relevant) on the *nature* of the source(s), i.e. who wrote it, what its purpose was, whether it is typical of the period. To do this properly, you will need to use your own knowledge to explain/evaluate the source(s) fully.

FactZONE

You need to learn these key facts:

Change and continuity in the Middle Ages

■ At first, in medieval Europe (and in the Islamic world), it was felt improper for male physicians to examine females, so female patients relied on other women. However, during the Middle Ages, the Church (which controlled education and the universities) began to make medical training more formal e.g. medical schools were set up. Even the training of **apothecaries** and **barber-surgeons** became more specialised. Women were excluded from most types of formal education, so only men were allowed to train as doctors.

■ The growing insistence on formal medical training began to squeeze women out of medicine, apart from **patient care**. Women who continued to practise medicine could be tried, e.g. **Jacoba de Felice** in 1322.

■ Women still played an important informal role for most people, acting as **midwives** (while some learnt their skills informally, others were more formally trained as apprentices and became members of a guild), and as **housewife-physicians** (often picking up a knowledge of plants and herbs from cooking and gardening).

■ As university-trained doctors were relatively scarce, and expensive, most ordinary people (especially in the countryside, where the majority lived) relied on these housewife-physicians and local **'wise women'**.

Developments after 1750

■ During the sixteenth and seventeenth centuries, increased knowledge and formal medical training at universities had excluded women from most areas of medicine. In about 1620, the **obstetric** (delivery) forceps had been invented – these required good anatomical knowledge to be used safely, so women were gradually excluded from midwifery.

■ In the eighteenth and nineteenth centuries, **social attitudes** worked against women being more than housewives and/or mothers. The number of female midwives, and even of herbalists (gradually replaced by male apothecaries and pharmacologists), declined. However, doctors were still scarce and expensive. As the population expanded during the Industrial Revolution, the poorer classes often relied on informal midwives and 'wise-women' for medical care.

■ The first signs of **change** came in **nursing,** following the work of **Florence Nightingale** during the Crimean War. But there were still no women doctors – women rarely had any secondary education, and universities and medical colleges refused to accept women as students. However, social attitudes concerning women's rights to education and employment began to change from about 1850.

■ Inspired by **Elizabeth Blackwell** (the first woman in the USA to qualify as a doctor, 1849), **Elizabeth Garrett** tried to qualify as a doctor in Britain. Though allowed (after a court case) to enrol in the Society of Apothecaries, no British university would allow her to qualify as a Doctor of Medicine (she eventually qualified in Paris, in 1870). **Sophia Jex-Blake** (and five other women) completed a full medical course at Edinburgh University in 1874, but the university said it could only award medical degrees to men (so they went to Dublin or Zurich to obtain degrees). They also set up the London School of Medicine for Women.

Examining sources for usefulness

📺 Change and continuity in the Middle Ages

Study the two sources below, which refer to the role of women in medicine during the Middle Ages.

Source A A medieval picture, showing a midwife delivering a baby by Caesarean section.

Source B An attack on women doctors by John of Mirfield, a physician at St Bartholomew's Hospital, London, during the fourteenth century.

> B
>
> Worthless and presumptuous women usurp this profession. Possessing neither natural ability nor professional knowledge, they make the greatest possible mistakes thanks to their stupidity, and very often kill the patients. For they work without wisdom and from no certain foundation of knowledge, but in a casual fashion.

 As well as discussing the nature, origin and purpose of the sources and what they show, think how you can use your own knowledge to indicate what the sources don't show.

❗ **REMEMBER** Make sure you comment on **all** the sources provided by the examiner and that you use your own knowledge.

❗ **REMEMBER** As this is a utility question, there is no need to comment at length about whether the sources are primary or secondary – don't try to turn it into a reliability question!

◎ *How useful are these two sources for showing the importance of women in medicine during the Middle Ages? Use your own knowledge, and the sources, to explain your answer.*

Source A shows a woman, assisted by another woman, carrying out a complicated operation - there is no man shown as being present. However, it might not be typical.

Source B refers to women 'usurping' (taking over) the 'profession' (not explained, but possibly midwifery). But it is written by a hostile male doctor (e.g. 'stupidity'), so might not be accurate/reliable about the abilities of women. However, it does suggest that many women were active in medicine.

From your own knowledge, it is important to show
(i) how most people were too poor to afford trained doctors, so they therefore relied on women (the 'housewife-physician', the 'wise women', as well as midwives) especially in rural areas, where the majority lived
(ii) how the Church, which controlled education and the medical profession, was gradually excluding women from the practice of medicine during the Middle Ages.

You could also comment on how the sources make no mention of women as herbalists or faith healers.

📺 Developments after 1750

Study the two sources below, which are both about the position of women in medicine in the period 1750-1900.

Source B A statement, made in 1861, by male students at the Middlesex Hospital, London.

Source A A cartoon of 1796, showing a male midwife.

A man – mid – wife.

> **B** We the undersigned students consider that the mixture of the sexes in the same class is likely to lead to results of an unpleasant character.
>
> The lecturers are likely to feel some restraint through the presence of females in giving that explicit and forcible enunciation of some facts which is necessary.
>
> The presence of young females as spectators in the operating theatre is an outrage on our natural instincts and feelings and calculated to destroy those sentiments of all right-minded men. Such feelings are a mark of civilisation and refinement.

❓ *Think about how the sources agree or differ, and try to show what the sources fail to say.*

◎ *Highlight any information given by the sources, and/or by the details of their origins.*

❗ **REMEMBER** Comment on the nature, origin and purpose of the sources, where relevant.

Practice question – developments after 1750

Study sources A and B, *and* use your own knowledge, to write three or four paragraphs to answer the following question. Allow yourself 20 minutes.

■ How useful are sources A and B in showing the position of women in medicine during the period 1750-1900?

To be able to answer questions on this topic, you will need to know something about the following:

• public health in the Middle Ages (collapse of the Roman Empire and organised public health; monasteries and hospitals; lack of government involvement; problems connected with the growth of towns; the Black Death – high death rate led the government to enforce certain measures, but there was no understanding of its causes, and hence of how to control it)

• continuing problems 1500-1750 (continued growth of population and towns; lack of government action; sixteenth- and seventeenth-century views and attitudes; the Great Plague of London, 1665-66).

• The Public Health Crisis, 1750-1850 (impact of the Industrial Revolution on urban housing and sanitation; infectious diseases, especially TB, typhus, typhoid and cholera; early government attitudes; Dr. Southwood-Smith, **Edwin Chadwick** and William Farr; the 1848 Public Health Act)

FACTORS:
Science and technology
Communications
Individuals
War
Government
Industry
Social attitudes

• developments 1850-1900 (opposition to reform; central government and local authorities; work of **John Snow**; impact of Pasteur's and Koch's discoveries; extension of the franchise, 1867; cholera epidemic, 1865-66; flushing toilets and Thomas Crapper; later reforms)

• changes since 1900 (impact of the Boer War; Liberal reforms 1906-14; effects of the First World War and the Depression; the Second World War and the NHS)

This section deals with public health in Britain, focusing on:

■ public health in the Middle Ages

■ the Public Health Crisis, 1750-1850

This section gives you practice at answering comprehension and recall questions. These require you to show you can understand and extract information from the sources, *and* use your own knowledge to add to the explanation or information provided by the source(s) concerning a particular event, situation or development.

FactZONE

You need to learn these key facts:

Public health in the Middle Ages

■ When the Roman Empire collapsed, practical measures for public health e.g. aqueducts for pure water, public toilets and baths, and draining of swamps, rapidly disappeared. Medieval governments were unwilling to provide public health facilities as they did not have the power, money or authority. Instead, each medieval town was left to itself, with decisions taken by the **corporation** (made up of rich men). Mostly, such corporations were reluctant to spend money, and felt it wasn't their responsibility.

■ While towns were small, there were no major public health problems. But as trade and towns grew, the potential risks increased. Often, rubbish and sewage piled up in the streets, or was dumped in nearby rivers.

■ Exceptions to this were the monasteries and church hospitals, which had kept alive aspects of Roman public health practices (e.g. water supply, cleanliness). But this benefited only a few. Although some towns passed by-laws (e.g. about the regular emptying of cesspits), these were difficult to enforce.

■ Usually, action only followed some serious outbreak of disease. The worst example was the **Black Death** (bubonic plague) which first hit Britain in 1348.

The Public Health Crisis 1750-1850

■ The rapid growth of population and towns during the Industrial Revolution led to worsened public health – overcrowded and bad housing, poor water supplies, inadequate drainage and sewerage. There were no planning or building regulations; most still believed that government should follow a **laissez-faire** policy (i.e. not interfere). Also, there was still no proper scientific/medical understanding of the causes of disease (theory of 'miasmas', or 'bad air').

■ As a result, there were real problems with infectious diseases (especially TB, typhus, and typhoid). Then, in 1831, a new disease hit Britain – **cholera**. Some boards of health were set up but were abolished in 1832, when the epidemic appeared to have died out. In 1839, the government, worried by the cholera epidemic, asked **Edwin Chadwick** to undertake an investigation into the links between poverty and ill-health. His Report, published in 1842, recommended sanitary reform and led to divided opinions in Parliament (the 'Clean' party versus the 'Dirty' party), and outside (a Health of Towns Association was set up in 1844).

■ Statistics, collected by **William Farr**, also showed the links between poverty, squalor and death rates - Chadwick's findings were also supported by those of **Dr. Southwood-Smith**. The 'Dirty' party of MPs defeated a Public Health Bill introduced in 1847 (they opposed the cost involved in cleaning up the towns; believed the poor - who didn't have the right to vote - should 'help themselves'; and pointed out that no one actually knew what caused these diseases).

■ But then cholera struck again in 1848. Parliament passed the **Public Health Act**. This allowed them to set up a General Board of Health, with local Boards of Health (if 10% of rate-payers agreed), which had the power to improve water supplies and sewage disposal (if they wanted to). However, this was not compulsory and so had limited results. Many water companies, landlords, builders and some doctors continued to oppose Chadwick's reforms.

Comprehension and recall questions

Public health in the Middle Ages

Study these two sources, which refer to the Black Death of 1348-49, and then answer the question which follows.

A *To the Lord Mayor of London*

An order to cause the human excreta and other filth lying in the streets and lanes in the city and its suburbs to be removed with all speed. Also to cause the city and suburbs to be kept clean, as it used to be in the time of the previous mayors. This is so that no greater cause of death may arise from such smells. The king has learnt that the city and suburbs are so full with filth from out of the houses by day and night that the air is infected and the city poisoned. This is a danger to men, especially by the contagious sickness which increases daily.

Source A An order sent by Edward III to the Lord Mayor of London in 1349, the year after the Black Death arrived in Britain.

Source B A fourteenth-century illustration of people whipping themselves (flagellants). They believed God had sent the Black Death because people were sinful and that by punishing themselves, they would persuade God to be merciful.

◎ *Using the two sources, and your own knowledge, explain what the main problems were concerning public health during the Middle Ages.*

◎ *Highlight the relevant points of information provided in the sources and/or by the details of their origins.*

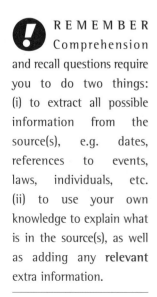

REMEMBER Comprehension and recall questions require you to do two things: (i) to extract all possible information from the source(s), e.g. dates, references to events, laws, individuals, etc. (ii) to use your own knowledge to explain what is in the source(s), as well as adding any **relevant** extra information.

Source A indicates lack of proper sewerage/sanitation in towns and suggests that the situation was worse than it used to be (and that it took a crisis to provoke government action). It also suggests that the Black Death ('contagious sickness') might be caused by 'bad smells'/'filth', etc., which shows lack of proper medical understanding.

Source B also shows an ignorance of the cause of the Black Death, hence ineffectual responses.

From your own knowledge, you could point out the decline in both knowledge/practical measures and government action since the fall of the Roman Empire; the growth of towns and problems of sanitation and water supply; and the fact that medical knowledge and scientific developments were not yet able to show links between dirt and ill-health etc.

📺 The Public Health Crisis 1750-1850

Study the two sources below, which refer to the cholera epidemic of 1831-32.

Source A An illustration of 1832, showing the washing of a cholera victim's bedclothes in the Mill Stream, Exeter (this was also the city's main source of drinking water).

B

The Board will at once see how the disease (cholera) has been rampant in those parts of the town where there is often an entire lack of sewerage, drainage and paving. In one division of the town occupied entirely by cottage dwellings, including cellar dwellings, for 386 persons there are but two single privies. In such streets as these the Board will see the highest rate of cholera attacks.

Source B Extract from the *Report to the Leeds Board of Health*, published in 1833, following a study of the cholera epidemic of 1831-32.

❗ **REMEMBER** From your own knowledge add further specific details and/or problems **not** mentioned (or only hinted at) by the sources.

◎ *Look carefully at your textbook and your notes before writing your answer.*

Practice question - the Public Health Crisis 1750-1850

Use the two sources above, and your own knowledge, to answer the following question. Allow yourself 20 minutes.

■ What were the major problems concerning public health in Britain during the period 1750-1850?

To be able to answer questions on this topic, you will need to know something about the following:

- the three problems of surgery – **pain, infection, bleeding**

- the state of surgery before 1800 (the work of Hugh of Lucca and his son, Theoderic, and of Paré, was largely ignored; barber-surgeons and surgeons lower than physicians)

- the discovery of anaesthetics (early 'anaesthetics'; **Humphrey Davy** and nitrous oxide or 'laughing gas', 1799; **John Warren** and ether, 1846; **James Simpson** and chloroform, 1847; problems and opposition; Queen Victoria uses chloroform, 1853; later developments)

- the discovery of antiseptics (the 'black period' of surgery; work of Ignaz Semmelweiss; Pasteur's germ theory and **Joseph Lister's** use of carbolic acid, 1867; problems and opposition; development of **aseptic surgery**)

- impact of the First World War (early work on blood transfusions, e.g. first human to human transfusion, 1818; **Karl Landsteiner** and blood groups, 1901; **Albert Hustin** and the development of anti-clotting agents and methods of blood storage, 1914-17; **Harold Gillies** and plastic surgery)

- impact of the Second World War (**Archibald McIndoe** and plastic surgery; **Dwight Harken** and heart surgery; stimulation of further research)

- modern 'high-tech' surgery (importance of discoveries and inventions, e.g. X-rays and Wilhelm Rontgen, 1895; electro-cardiograph and Willem Einthoven, 1903; artificial kidney machine and Willem Kolff, 1943; fibre optics and 'key-hole' surgery; transplants and micro-surgery)

FACTORS:
Science and technology
Communications
Individuals
War

This section deals with surgery since 1750, focusing on:

■ the discovery of antiseptics

■ the impact of the Second World War

This section gives you practice at answering cause and consequence questions. Such questions require you to show, by the use of relevant knowledge of your own, the role of a factor (e.g. chance, science, war) in bringing about a change or discovery that results in progress or an advance being made.

FactZONE

You need to learn these key facts:

The discovery of antiseptics

■ Though the discovery of anaesthetics had removed the problem of pain from surgery (so allowing longer, more complex operations), operations were still carried out in **unhygienic conditions** (no clean, special clothes for surgeons, no sterilisation of instruments etc. between operations). Death rates from operations actually rose. The period 1846-70 is known as the 'black period' of surgery. In 1847, **Dr. Ignaz Semmelweiss**, working in Vienna, ordered doctors to wash their hands (in chloride of lime) before examining patients. (Doctors often dissected bodies and then immediately examined women who had given birth.)

■ However, though Semmelweiss' method led to a dramatic decrease in deaths from puerperal fever, most doctors rejected his ideas. In 1861, Pasteur's **germ theory** was published. It was read and applied by **Joseph Lister**, who began, in 1865, to study the infection of wounds. In 1867, he used **carbolic acid** to disinfect bandages. Then he developed a **carbolic spray**, used on surgeon's hands, instruments, patients and the air from 1871. It was a **breakthrough**, and this method of **antiseptics** led to dramatic decreases in deaths from septic wounds (as well as a great increase in the numbers, and cost, of operations).

■ But many doctors and nurses disliked the new method (it affected their hands and lungs, and meant more work). However, the earlier successes of Florence Nightingale in the Crimean War gradually led to better-trained nurses willing to use the new methods. Also, there was slow acceptance of Pasteur's ideas, until Koch's discovery in 1878 of the bacteria causing infection.

■ The next breakthrough came in 1887 in Germany, with the discovery of **asepsis** techniques by Professor **Neuber** and **Ernst Bergmann** - this kept germs away altogether, rather than killing them, by sterilising clothes and instruments via superheated **steam**. In 1889 in the USA, **William S. Halsted** developed the idea of rubber gloves, caps, masks and gowns, to protect patients, nurses and doctors.

The impact of the Second World War

■ During the First World War, apart from important developments in blood transfusions, work had also seriously begun in a new specialism – plastic surgery – needed because of the horrific wounds to soldiers' faces etc. caused by new weapons. **Harold Gillies**, in Britain, had been the first plastic surgeon to consider the patients' appearance. His assistant, **Archibald McIndoe**, set up a unit in East Grinstead during the Second World War, treating airmen disfigured by blazing petrol. He used developments in drugs (sulphonamides and penicillin) to prevent infection. Plastic surgery has gone on to become an important specialism in surgery for all suffering from injuries or birth defects.

■ During the Second World War, another specialism progressed – heart surgery. Attempts at heart surgery before the war were rare, and not very successful – lungs collapsed and the heart stopped when touched. US army surgeon, Dwight Harken, cut into beating hearts and used his fingers to remove bullets and shrapnel. His successes in operating on injured hearts stimulated further research and so speeded up developments in open heart surgery e.g. Norman Shumway, at the University of Minnesota, and Michael de Blakey at the Methodist Hospital in Houston, Texas.

Cause and consequence questions

📺 The discovery of antiseptics

Study these two sources, which relate to the work of Florence Nightingale during the Crimean War 1854-56, and then answer the question below.

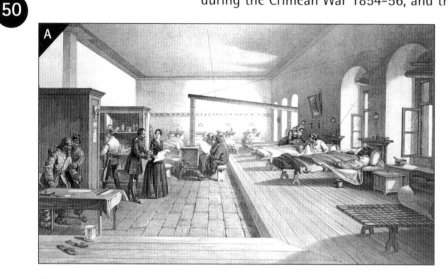

Source A A ward in the military hospital at Scutari, after it had been cleaned and reorganised by Florence Nightingale and her nurses.

Nightingale had high hopes that her success in the Crimea would enable her to establish nursing as a respected profession. In 1859 she published a book called *Notes on Nursing* which described her methods. It stressed the importance of professionalism and ward hygiene and became the standard text for trainee nurses.

A public fund was opened to enable Nightingale to develop the training of nurses. It raised £44,000 and the money was used to start up the Nightingale School of Nursing at St Thomas's Hospital in London. It was here that the standards were laid down for the training of nurses.

Source B Extract from a school history textbook, published in 1996.

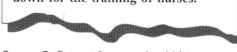

(?) *Think carefully about the question, as it is asking you to do several things. You need to choose and describe something that was done and explain its link to advances/progress in surgery.*

◎ *Using sources A and B above, and your own knowledge, give ONE example from Florence Nightingale's work to show how experience in war contributed to advances made in surgery during the nineteenth century.*

Source A's caption refers to **cleanliness** – something Florence Nightingale stressed. (This was before the work of Pasteur – she knew nothing about germs or germ theory).

Source B refers to **hygiene**, and to professionalism and **training** for nurses.

From your own knowledge, consider that Florence Nightingale had great success in reducing the death rate at Scutari hospital (from 42% to 2%), because of her stress on **hygiene/cleanliness**, and so helped pave the way for acceptance of Lister's later use of antiseptics. She stressed the proper **training** of nurses (e.g. the Nightingale School for Nurses). This meant that, after Lister's discovery, there were educated nurses able to use antiseptics (and other new methods), so allowing the more complicated surgical operations (made possible by anaesthetics and antiseptics) to have greater success rates.

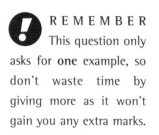

❗ REMEMBER This question only asks for **one** example, so don't waste time by giving more as it won't gain you any extra marks.

Impact of the Second World War

Study the two sources below, which refer to developments in surgery during the Second World War.

Source A A painting showing Archibald McIndoe and his team operating in 1944 on a patient disfigured by blazing petrol.

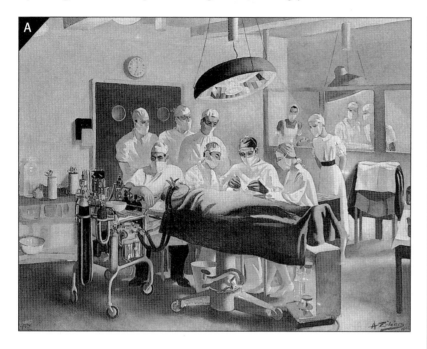

B The Second World War provided the stimulus to further research as some soldiers had bullets and fragments of shrapnel lodged in their hearts. A US army surgeon, Dwight Harken, had the courage to try to save them. He cut into the beating heart and stuck in his fingers to remove the fragment. This made little difference to most patients who needed open heart surgery to correct defects. The problem was that the blood supply needed to be cut off when the heart was opened. After four minutes, this caused brain damage.

(?) *Consider how you can **show** the link between the development you have selected and described, and its significance for advances in surgery in later decades.*

(?) *Think carefully about the wording of your answer. Try to use words and phrases such as 'this meant that ...', 'so ...' or 'therefore ...'. These are good link words to show the examiner that you have clearly seen the **significance/ importance** of the example you have selected. Look at the page opposite to see these 'link' words.*

Source B An extract describing the work of Dwight Harken, taken from a school textbook, published in 1996.

Practice question – the impact of the Second World War

Write two paragraphs to answer this question. Allow yourself 10 minutes.

■ 'Using Sources A and B, and your own knowledge, give ONE example to show how experience in the Second World War contributed to the advances made in 'high tech' surgery after 1945.

The Plains Indians

To be able to answer questions on this topic, you will need to know something about the following:

• the Great Plains (geography, environment)

• the Native Americans or American Indians (population, movements, settlement of the Plains; the 'Permanent Indian Frontier' of the 1830s – west of 95th meridian line in 1834)

• the different nations of the Plains Indians (organisation; warfare; weapons: lances, bows and arrows, tomahawks, and stone-headed or war clubs)

• the Plains Indians' way of life (hunting and nomadic lifestyle; roles of men, women and children)

• the importance of the buffalo (food, clothing, shelter, fuel, tools; importance to culture and religion).

• the Plains Indians' beliefs (attitude to the environment and nature, religion)

This section deals with the Plains Indians, focusing on:

■ the different nations of the Plains Indians

■ the Plains Indians' beliefs

This section gives you practice at answering comprehension in context questions. Such questions require you to extract information from the source(s) and to use your own knowledge about the topic to add to what is given by the sources(s).

You need to learn these key facts:

The different nations of the Plains Indians

■ **Nations** were large groups of Native Americans, each speaking a different language.

■ The five most important nations of the Great Plains were the:

| Sioux | Comanche | Crow | Cheyenne | Apache |

Also important were the: Arapaho
Kiowa

■ These nations were divided into different **tribes**. Each tribe consisted of several **bands**, made up of different families, containing between 100 and 500 people.

■ Each band had a **chief** and a council of **elders**, but all decisions had to be agreed by *all* the men.

■ Several of these nations were often allies: for example, the Sioux, Cheyenne and Arapaho, and the Comanche, Kiowa and Apache.

■ However, wars between nations were also common: success in war was of particular importance to each tribe, as well as to individual warriors.

■ There were strict codes of honour in warfare: wars were short, fierce battles to steal horses or to win honour by 'counting coup'. The intention was *not* to defeat other tribes or take their lands.

■ Scalping sometimes took place, partly as proof of success in battle, but mainly to avoid meeting an enemy in the after-life.

The Plains Indians' beliefs

■ All Native Americans, especially the Plains Indians, believed that land was sacred and so could not be bought, sold or fenced off. '

■ The various nations had different creation beliefs. Some believed in one 'Father of Life' or 'The Great Spirit', but all believed that each creature had a place in nature. Therefore, it was wrong to kill more than you needed, or to pollute the environment.

■ They believed all elements of the natural world were connected and contained spirits. As all living things were holy, they did not believe humans were more important than other creatures.

■ They belived that as their ancestors had died and become dust on the plains, the land was sacred to their tribe.

■ They believed nature worked in circles – the sun, the seasons, and life itself. So circles became important symbols – tepees were round, villages were built in circles, and even dances took the form of a circle.

■ Medicine men and ceremonial and religious dances were very important – all were based on the worship of nature and its spirits.

Comprehension in context questions

⊡ The different nations of the Plains Indians

Study the two sources below, which are about the nature of warfare amongst the Plains Indians.

Source A An extract from a book about the Cheyenne, published in 1978.

Source B A picture, painted in 1892, showing an Indian scalping a dead soldier.

A

War has been transformed into a great game in which scoring against the enemy often takes precedence over killing him. The scoring is in the counting of coup – touching or striking an enemy with hand or weapons...
A man's rank as a warrior depends on two factors: his total 'score' in coups, and his ability to lead successful raids in which Cheyenne losses are low. Actual killing and scalping get their credit, too, but they do not rate as highly as the show-off deeds.

❗ REMEMBER
For this type of question, you need to do two things: extract as much information as possible from the source(s) e.g. dates, references to events/practices/ laws/individuals, etc.; and use your own knowledge of the topic to add to, and explain, what is and what isn't in the source(s).

◉ *Do these two sources show that the Plains Indians' methods of warfare were completely different from those of the white settlers?*

Source A mentions the importance of 'counting coup' against an enemy. This was even more important than killing him. It also stresses the idea of keeping casualties low, and the practice of scalping.

Source B confirms the practice of scalping.

From your own knowledge mention that counting coup *was* different, as was the preference for avoiding large-scale battles. Also note that neither of the two sources mentions white methods of warfare. However, whites sometimes scalped the Indians they killed.

📺 The Plains Indians' beliefs

Study these two sources, which are two extracts about Sioux beliefs concerning nature and the environment.

A

Kinship with all the creatures of the earth, sky and water was a real and active principle. For the animal and bird world there existed a brotherly feeling that kept the Lakota safe among them and so close did some of the Lakota come to their feathered and furred friends that in true brotherhood they spoke a common tongue.

Source A Standing Bear's explanation of how the Sioux viewed the world.

B

You have noticed that everything the Indian does is in a circle and that is because the Power of the World always works in circles, and everything tries to be round. In the old days when we were a strong and happy people, all our powers came to us from the sacred hoop of the nation, and so long as the hoop was unbroken, the people flourished. The flowering tree was the living centre of the hoop, and the circle of the four quarters nourished it. The east gave peace and light, the south gave warmth, the west gave rain and the north with its cold and mighty wind gave strength and endurance.

Source B How Black Elk, a Sioux medicine man, explained the importance of circles.

❓ *Consider what the two sources tell us about the beliefs of the Plains Indians.*

❓ *Think how you can use your own knowledge to give a fuller explanation (there are several aspects not covered).*

◎ *Highlight the information given by the sources, and/or by the details of their origins.*

Practice question – the Plains Indians' beliefs

Use the sources, *and* your own knowledge, to answer the following question. Allow yourself 15 minutes.

■ Do these two sources give us enough information to understand the Plains Indians' attitudes to nature?

To be able to answer questions on this topic, you will need to know something about the following:

- the pioneers (fur trappers and traders, mountain men; the American Fur Company and the Hudson's Bay Company; collapse of the fur trade)

- the opening up of the West (missionaries; land shortage and the 1837 financial crisis in the East; government support)

- trailblazers and wagon trains (numbers; hazards; the Oregon Trail; relations with Plains Indians; white settlements)

- the Mormons (leaders, beliefs, reasons for the move West, Salt Lake City)

- impact of mining (California Gold Rush; early miners and towns; conditions; growth of mining corporations)

- developments in transport and communications (steamboats, stage coaches, the Pony Express, telegraph)

- the coming of the railroads (government backing; the Central Pacific and Union Pacific Railroads: problems and progress; effect on the way of life of the Plains Indians (e.g. disruption of buffalo hunting, growing conflict, increasing involvement of US army)

- impact of the railroads on development of the West (larger cities, growth of cow towns, prosperity for homesteaders, improved law and education)

This section deals with pioneers, early settlers and transport, focusing on:

- trailblazers and wagon trains
- the coming of the railroads

This section gives you practice at answering questions which require you to analyse the factors associated with a particular change or development.

To answer such questions, you will need to use any relevant knowledge of your own to support your analysis or argument. You may also have to refer to a source or sources. You will certainly have to deal with a *range* of factors, deciding, where appropriate, which were more and which were less important.

You need to learn these key facts:

Trailblazers and wagon trains

■ Many fur-trappers and mountain men also helped 'blaze' the first trails (routes) across the Great Plains (e.g. James P. Beckwourth, Kit Carson, Jim Bridger).

■ These trailblazers opened up the West for the huge wave of settlers who followed them - along the **Santa Fe Trail** (Joseph Walker), and especially the **Oregon Trail** (Jedediah Smith and John Charles Fremont).

■ In 1843, the **great migration** began when 913 people left Independence, Missouri to travel 3200km to Oregon. In 1844 (as part of **'Manifest Destiny'** and their campaign to encourage settlers to go West), the US government printed 10 000 copies of the map of the Oregon Trail made by Fremont in 1843-44.

■ By then, land was scarce in the East and the 1837 financial crisis had ruined many businesses and hit farming. Land was cheaper in the West, and the government promised land to settlers.

■ As a result, thousands more crossed the Great Plains in the 1840s to make a new life in Oregon or California (which became part of the USA in 1846 and 1848 respectively). By 1848, nearly 15 000 settlers had gone West.

■ Most travelled in covered wagons, as part of a **wagon train** led by a pilot and his scout. There were many hazards (weather, disease, buffalo stampedes, shortages of food and water). To avoid winter blizzards, most journeys began in late April/early May. Progress was slow, about fifteen miles a day, so journeys took about four and a half months.

■ At first, most Indian tribes traded with the early white migrants, but when the number of settlers increased, tensions grew. The US government then sent troops to protect the settlers, and built forts along the trails.

The coming of the railroads

■ After defeating Mexico and taking California in 1848, nationalism increased in the USA. 'Manifest Destiny' led the government to subsidise mapping, shipping and stage-coach lines. As settlers and miners in the West increased, a **transcontinental railroad** was proposed. It received strong government support as it was seen as a way of uniting the country.

■ The US army began surveying possible routes for the railroad. However, the American Civil War closed off southern routes, so a central route was chosen. Two companies were set up:

■ **the Central Pacific Railroad** (starting in California)
■ **the Union Pacific Railroad** (starting in Omaha)

The government helped by giving generous loans, grants, and land next to the tracks (often sold to settlers). Routes through mountains were difficult – large numbers of Chinese workers were brought in (they suffered bad treatment and prejudice). Once the Civil War ended in 1865, more workers (often Irish) came West. Temporary shanty towns grew up (similar to mining camps).

■ On 10 May 1869, at the **Golden Spike Ceremony**, the two lines met at Promontory Point, Utah. From 1870, several more lines were built in the West.

Analysis of change questions

📺 Trailblazers and wagon trains

Study the source below, which is a map showing the main trails west in 1840.

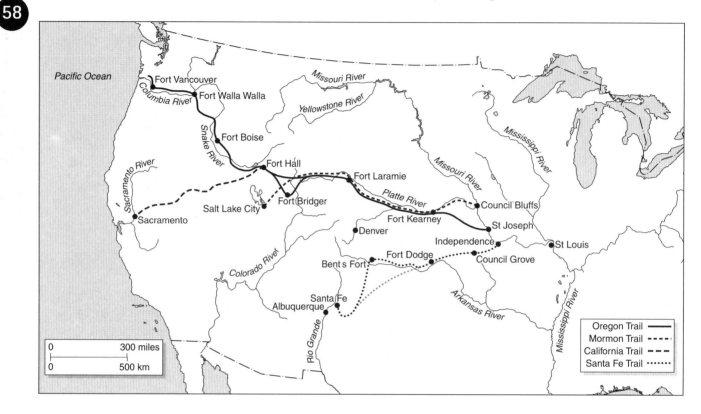

! **REMEMBER** This a question about change, so you will be expected to identify several different elements or key features of **change**. You will only get low marks if you simply tell the story of what the trailblazers did.

◎ *How did the opening up of the first trails by the early trailblazers affect the development of the West?*

⑦ *Consider how you can show a **detailed** knowledge of the impact or effect of the trails on the West. If the information is general (e.g. 'They enabled/encouraged more settlers to go West'), you will only get low marks.*

With questions like this, it is a good idea to compile a list of rough points. You can then add more detailed knowledge. The main features you could identify would include:

■ the early problems of moving West (getting lost)

■ how the early trails encouraged more settlers and miners to move West (1843: less than 1000; by 1848: 15 000)

■ impact on the Great Plains and the Plains Indians (homesteads, miners' towns, disruption of Indians' way of life – buffalo, disease).

📺 The coming of the railroads

Study the source below, which is a photograph showing the building of a railroad.

Chinese workers on the Central Pacific Railroad.

❓ *Think about what **detailed** knowledge of your own you can use to add to the general points you can make.*

❓ *Consider the question carefully. To **show change**, you will need to give information about what the situation was like **before** and **after**. Also, assess whether some changes were more significant than others.*

◎ *Try to make a rough list of the changes, and then add in detailed and precise knowledge of your own, to illustrate the changes to which you refer.*

❗ **REMEMBER** You should make **change** the basis of your answer – this is not an invitation merely to describe all you know about the building of the railroads.

Practice question – the coming of the railroads

Write three or four paragraphs to answer the question. Allow yourself 20 minutes.

■ In what ways did the railroads change the way of life of the Plains Indians?

Cattle, ranchers and homesteaders

To be able to answer questions on this topic, you will need to know something about the following:

• Texas and the early cattle industry

• the effects of the Civil War and railroads

• cattle trails and cattle towns (Sedalia Trail; Goodnight-Loving Trail; Chisholm Trail and Joseph G McCoy; Abilene and Dodge City; reactions of Native Americans; Jayhawkers)

• ranching on the Great Plains (increase in numbers, the open range, refrigeration, hardier breeds)

• the life and work of cowboys (myth and reality: dress and equipment, the Long Drive, hazards, working and living conditions)

• cattle barons and the end of the open range (cost of fencing; end of the cattle boom; the winter of 1886-87)

• farming and life on the Great Plains (hopes of settlers; early problems of farming; women's lives)

• effects of Government Acts and the railroads (Homestead Act, 1862 and its problems; Timber Culture Act, 1873; Desert Land Act, 1877)

• later developments from the 1870s onwards (barbed wire, wind pumps, dry farming techniques, new crop varieties, new farm machinery)

This section deals with cattle, ranchers and homesteaders, focusing on:

■ the life and work of cowboys

■ farming and life on the Great Plains

This section tests your ability to use a source or sources, and your own knowledge, to identify the key features of a particular historical issue or problem. Such answers should do more than simply mention the problem(s). Try to expand on the problem(s), using your own knowledge to briefly indicate how these were resolved.

You need to learn these key facts.

The life and work of cowboys

■ Cowboys first came from Texas, where the cattle industry began. Later, they came from all over the USA. After the Civil War, they included black veterans of the Unionist army and ex-slaves.

■ The **Long Drive** was the movement of cattle north along the lengthy cattle trails to the railheads. Life on the Long Drive was hard, with low wages and poor food. Work began at dawn, and carried on until the hottest part of the day, when the cattle were watered and grazed. As the heat subsided, the cattle were moved on. There was also night duty.

■ The main **hazards** were stampedes, river crossings, sun, blizzards, drought, dust, and Indian attacks or raids. There were also conflicts with homesteaders, and white rustlers or robbers (Jayhawkers).

■ Despite low pay, the clothes and equipment needed (boots, chaps and especially saddles) could be very expensive, and had to be provided by the men themselves.

■ The Long Drive was often very different from the romantic picture painted by some. It often took up to four months to travel from Texas to Abilene. Often, the long hours, dangers and boredom resulted in quarrels.

■ As cattle ranching spread in the 1860s and 1870s, some cowboys became more settled and worked on one ranch. However, the work was still hard, long, unglamorous and low paid: in 1883, cowboys in Texas went on strike for better pay.

Farming and life on the Great Plains

■ From the 1860s onwards, large numbers of people settled on the Great Plains, for various reasons: land was scarce in the East, people were seeking a more prosperous life or trying to make a new life after the Civil War. By 1895, there were nearly 450 000 homesteads in the new Western territories.

■ The government aided settlement. Although there were problems with the Homestead Act of 1862, later acts in 1873 and 1877 partly solved them.

■ There were many problems on the Great Plains: shortage of timber for houses meant many lived in **dugouts** or **sod houses**. These attracted insects, were damp and were impossible to keep clean (but were warm in winter, cool in summer).

■ Other difficulties included lack of water (it was hard to dig wells); poor soil; problems with insects; extreme variations in climate (floods, droughts, 'twisters', snow).

■ Women had many responsibilities: looking after children, cleaning and decorating the house, making and washing clothes, cooking, growing vegetables, tending smaller animals. At busy times, women were also expected to help with the heavier farming work.

■ All tasks were very time-consuming: it took a whole day just to do the family laundry. There was no running water, and women even had to make their own soap. All cooking was done at the fireplace - women had to collect buffalo chips (dung) for fuel.

■ Life was very isolated. Doctors were very scarce at first, childbirth was often faced alone, etc.

Recall and analysis of key features

⊕ The life and work of cowboys

Look at the source below, which is a painting by Frederic Remington depicting a stampede.

Longhorn cattle stampede due to a flash of lightning.

 REMEMBER As this question refers to problems, it is a good idea to jot down, in rough, all the points you can remember, before you begin. In this way, you should be certain of scoring maximum points.

◎ *Using the source, and your own knowledge, describe the main problems faced by cowboys on the Long Drive.*

To answer this question, make sure you refer to the source, which shows one of the hazards experienced by cowboys on the cattle trails.

You should also make sure you write about other problems. Don't take too long on this if the question only carries three or four marks. However, make sure you mention about three or four different points.

◎ *List the main problems without looking at the Factzone. Then check back to see if you have missed anything.*

📺 Farming and life on the Great Plains

Look at the source below, which is a photograph of a white woman and child on a Kansas homestead.

Collecting buffalo dung for fuel.

(?) *Think carefully about the lives of women homesteaders, then write down, in rough, a list of points. You can then expand on them in your answer.*

❗ REMEMBER
The question only asks about the lives of women on homesteads in the Great Plains, so **don't** write about the general problems of living on homesteads, or the problems of Plains Indian women.

Practice question – farming and life on the Great Plains

Write five or six sentences to answer the question, making sure to refer to the source above. Allow yourself 15 minutes.

■ What was life like for women on homesteads on the Great Plains?

To be able to answer questions on this topic, you will need to know something about the following:

- the difficulties in policing US federal territories (large areas, distance from Washington, slowness of transport, shortage of suitable law enforcement officers)

- disorder in both mining camps and towns and the cow towns (Tombstone, Deadwood, miners' courts; Abilene, Dodge City and Newton)

- early law enforcers (US marshals, sheriffs and posses; vigilance committees, vigilante groups and lynchings; Texas Rangers, private detective agencies)

- gunslingers and outlaw gangs (e.g. Butch Cassidy, the Sundance Kid and the Wild Bunch; Jesse James and the James – Younger Gang; Billy the Kid. There were also several women outlaws, e.g. Belle Starr, Etta Place [part of the Wild Bunch], 'Cattle Annie' McDougal, Jennie 'Little Breeches' Metcalf)

- conflict on the range (cattlemen versus homesteaders, Range Wars)

- end of the 'wild' West (railways and the telegraph; increased population; federal territories become self-governing states)

This section deals with law and order in the West, focusing on:

- gunslingers and outlaw gangs
- conflict on the range

This section gives you practice at answering causation questions. These require you to use your own knowledge to describe and analyse the importance of the different key features behind a particular historical event or development. Do not merely present a list of factors – try to show how a range of reasons combined together. Also, if possible, try to decide if some of the factors are more important than others.

You need to learn these key facts:

Gunslingers and outlaw gangs

■ Problems of distance and travel in the West made it relatively easy for those wishing to rob or murder.

■ The situation was made worse by the lack of suitable law enforcement officers. Even famous lawmen, such as Wyatt Earp, sometimes had dubious careers. People like Bill Tilghman were rare – many sheriffs took bribes or even committed crimes themselves (such as Henry Plummer and his gang, known as the Innocents).

■ Sometimes, wealthy cattlemen hired gunslingers in their disputes with homesteaders.

■ However, the West was probably not as wild as novels and films have made it seem. Much of the killing was between rival criminals, and both gunslingers, and their biographers, often exaggerated their exploits.

Conflict on the range

Conflict between cattlemen and homesteaders developed for several reasons:

■ in the early days, cattle roamed freely on the open range, and frequently destroyed the homesteaders' crops
■ disputes arose over access to water and water rights
■ as cattlemen moved to establishing permanent ranches, arguments developed over land ownership and staked claims.

Such disputes often became violent. At times, these developed into full-scale range wars. Two of the most famous were:

■ **The Lincoln County War, 1877–81**. This was between **John Chisum**, the owner of a large ranch in Lincoln County, New Mexico, and **Lawrence Murphy**, who owned a much smaller ranch.

■ **The Johnson County War, 1892**. In the late 1880s, the cattle boom ended because of over-production and the blizzards of the winter of 1886-87. The cattle barons blamed their troubles on the small ranchers and homesteaders whose barbed wire fences had ended the open range.

■ The cattle barons in Johnson County, Wyoming formed the Wyoming Stock Growers' Association and, in 1888, got a local law passed known as the Maverick Bill. In 1889, two homesteaders, Jim Averill and Ella Watson, were lynched. More murders occurred in 1891. The cattlemen then hired a private army, known as the **Regulators**.

■ Though homesteader **Nate Champion** was gunned down, the settlers fought back, and the Regulators had to be rescued by the US cavalry. None of the cattle barons or Regulators were convicted, but the power of the cattle barons was broken.

Causation questions

Gunslingers and outlaw gangs

Study the source below, which is a photograph of Billy the Kid.

! **REMEMBER**
This type of question asks you to examine and analyse the causes or reasons behind a historical event or situation, not simply describe something.

◎ *Why were gunfighters and outlaw gangs able to operate so openly in the 'wild' West?*

❓ *Try to think of as wide a range of relevant factors as possible: you will not get top marks if you only write about one or two causes. Also, consider whether it is possible to identify one or two of the factors as being more important than the others.*

Try to make a rough list of the main points **before** looking at the Factzone. Such a list should include:

■ the huge size of the Great Plains made it difficult to control law and order
■ lack of reliable law enforcers
■ Plains dwellers reluctant to pay taxes for policing
■ most people carried guns
■ operation of vigilante groups
■ conflict between cattle barons and homesteaders

Conflict on the range

Study the source below, which is about the event of 1889 that helped start the Johnson County War.

An artist's impression of the lynching of Ella Watson and James Averill, 1889.

REMEMBER
This is a question which asks you to explain **why** something happened, so don't just describe a series of events.

Think how you can use your own knowledge to build up a range of different causes or factors. You might find it helpful to make a rough list first and to identify those factors which you think were more/less important.

Practice question – conflict on the range

Use your own knowledge to answer the following question. Allow yourself 25 minutes.

■ Explain why cattlemen came into conflict with homesteaders in the American West.

To be able to answer questions on this topic, you will need to know something about the following:

• the clash of cultures on the Great Plains (differing ideas about land ownership, nature and the environment; different lifestyles)

• the changing attitudes and policies of the federal government and whites (the Great Plains as 'Wilderness'; the 'Permanent Indian Frontier' (1830-34); expansion of USA westwards; nationalism and the desire for one united county)

• the early conflict on the Great Plains (the new US nation spread further west in the 1840s: Oregon was ceded by Britain in 1846, and California was taken, in 1848, after the war with Mexico; increased numbers of homesteaders [Oregon Trail] and miners [California Gold Rush] seriously disrupted the Indian way of life, especially by buffalo hunting and the spread of European diseases; 'Manifest Destiny' and the 'Indian Problem'; **Fort Laramie Treaty**, 1851 and reservations)

• the Plains Wars, 1854-68 (the Grattan Incident, 1854; Little Crow's War, 1862; **Fort Wise (Fort Lyon) Treaty**, 1861; the Cheyenne Uprising, 1863-67, and the **Medicine Lodge Creek Treaty**, 1867; the Bozeman Trail, Red Cloud's War, 1867-68, and the **Fort Laramie Treaty**, 1868; the 'Winter Campaign' against the Cheyenne, 1868)

• the Plains Wars, 1869-90 (the 'Great Plains Massacre' of the buffalo; the Red River War, 1874-75; War for the Black Hills, 1875-77; the Dawes Act, 1887; the Ghost Dance and Massacre at Wounded Knee)

This section deals with the defeat of the Plains Indians, focusing on:

■ early conflict on the Great Plains

■ the Plains Wars, 1869-90

This section gives you practice at answering questions which test your ability to assess the reliability of sources.

To decide how reliable sources are, you need to examine the kind of source it is, who wrote it (or took the photograph etc.), its purpose, any possible bias, and whether it is a typical or unrepresentative view.

You need to learn these key facts:

Early conflict on the Great Plains

By the late 1840s, some Indians had begun to attack wagon trains and settlers. This **'Indian Problem'** resulted in the US army being sent in. The theory of **'Manifest Destiny'** was used to justify white settlement of the Great Plains.

The Fort Laramie Treaty, 1851, forced the Plains Indians to give up their unlimited right to roam the Great Plains and to accept routes through their territory. In return, each nation had its own lands (which whites could not enter), along with gifts and an annual payment (ten years, later reduced to five). But many Indians resented the restrictions on traditional hunting.

Of the two government bodies dealing with Native Americans, the **War Department** was more hostile than the **Indian Bureau** – most senior army officers (Sherman, Sheridan, Custer, Chivington) were extremely prejudiced against Indians.

The US government began to move away from a policy of 'one large reservation' to **concentration** on smaller reservations. They made no serious attempts to prevent white settlers from breaking the 1851 Treaty almost immediately.

The Plains Wars, 1869-90

By the end of the 1860s, recent treaties – **Medicine Lodge Creek Treaty**, 1867 (with the Cheyenne, Arapaho, Comanche and Kiowa) and **Fort Laramie Treaty**, 1868 (with the Sioux) were already being broken, and life on the reservations was increasingly difficult (poor land, limited hunting, corrupt agents).

From the early 1870s, the government supported the wholesale slaughter of the buffalo (**'The Great Plains Massacre'**) as a way of forcing Indians to accept new terms. This led to the final stages of the defeat of the Plains Indians.

The Red River War 1874-75. The mass slaughter of buffalo alarmed the Plains Indians, and led to limited conflicts, 1870-74. The Kiowa (led by **Santana**) and the Comanche (led by **Quanah Parker**) then began their 'war to save the buffalo'. Their defeat marked the end of resistance in the south and central Great Plains.

The War for the Black Hills 1875-77. In the north, the Fort Laramie Treaty of 1868 had created a Great Sioux Reservation which included the **Bighorn Mountains** and the **Black Hills of Dakota**. But, in 1874, gold was discovered in the Black Hills – miners went in and the government tried to re-negotiate the 1868 Treaty.

The Sioux refused, and leadership passed to **Sitting Bull** and **Crazy Horse**, who had never accepted the 1868 Treaty. Despite defeating Custer in the **Battle of the Little Bighorn** in 1876, the Sioux were eventually forced to return to their reservations.

Life on the reservations was made even worse by the **Dawes (General Allotments) Act**, 1887. By 1890, in desperation, many followed **Wovoka's Ghost Dance** idea. The authorities were alarmed: the **Massacre at Wounded Knee**, in December 1890, ended the Ghost Dance. The Plains Wars were effectively over.

Source reliability questions

📺 Early conflict on the Great Plains

Look at the two sources below, which relate to events on the Great Plains in the 1840s and 1850s.

A

They are in terrible want of food half the year. The travel upon the road [trail] drives the buffalo off or else confines them to a narrow path during the period of migration...
their women are pinched with want and their children are constantly crying with hunger.

Source A Part of a report, made in 1853, by the Indian Agent for the Upper Platte and Arkansas River Country, on the effect of wagon trains on the Oregon Trail on the life of the Plains Indians.

B

Scarcely were the refugees settled behind the security of the 'permanent Indian frontier' when soldiers began marching westward through the Indian country. When the War with Mexico ended in 1847, the United States took possession of a vast expanse of territory, reaching from Texas to California. All of it was west of the 'permanent Indian frontier'.

In 1848 gold was discovered in California. Within a few months, fortune-seeking easterners by the thousand were crossing the Indian Territory... Most of them were bound for California gold, but some turned southwest for New Mexico or northwest for Oregon country. To justify these breaches of the 'permanent Indian frontier', the policy makers in Washington invented Manifest Destiny...

Source B Extract from a history book published in 1970.

❗ REMEMBER When answering reliability questions you must comment in detail on the **author**, the possible **purpose** of the source and the **nature** of the source.

 Think how you can use your own knowledge of the period to explain your choice.

◎ *Highlight points provided in the sources, and/or in the information about their origins.*

◎ *Which of these two sources would you choose as being more reliable for showing why the Plains Indians were unhappy about developments on the Great Plains in the period 1840-51?*

Source A is a report written by a US government agent – it was probably not intended for publication so it is more likely to be truthful. The author is also probably writing from first-hand observation. *But* the date is 1853 – the situation might not have been the same in 1840-51. It is also only one man's view of one area of the Great Plains, so it might not be *typical*.

Source B is a secondary source, by an historian, presumably with access to a wide range of historical sources. The account should be more balanced, and the language is not emotive (therefore not biased?). It also refers to the late 1840s so coincides with the dates in the question.

From your own knowledge, you can see that source A's comments match negative effect of wagon trains on buffalo hunting, on which the Indians depended. Source B also confirms the impact of the Oregon Trail, but in additon, mentions other factors (gold, 'Manifest Destiny', and breaches of 'Permanent Indian Frontier'). Overall, therefore, Source B seems more reliable.

📺 The Plains Wars, 1869–90

Study the two sources here, which are different impressions of the Sioux and Cheyenne defeat of General Custer at the Battle of the Little Bighorn, 1876.

Source A A painting by E.S. Paxson, made in 1899.

Source B An impression by Kicking Bear, a Sioux warrior in the battle.

❗ REMEMBER
If the question asks you to use your own knowledge and/or to make a choice between sources, make sure you do just that. Do not simply list the positive and negative features of each source in turn.

❓ *When answering the practice question below, think how you can comment on the sources:*

- *nature: what kind of sources are they?*
- *origin: who produced the sources?*
- *purpose: what were the likely purpose(s) of the sources?*

Practice question – the Plains Wars, 1869–90

Write three or four paragraphs to answer the following question. Allow yourself 20 minutes.

- Which of the two sources above is more reliable for showing what happened during Custer's 'Last Stand' in 1876? Use your knowledge of the event to help explain your choice.

To be able to answer questions on this topic, you will need to know something about the following:

• the end of the First World War

• revolution in Germany (abdication of the Kaiser; role of Ebert, elected President of the new German republic in February 1919, and the SPD (Social Democrats); the Spartacists and the Freikorps)

• the Weimar Republic and its constitution (drawn up in Weimar and accepted in August 1919; however, Germany was not used to democracy, as democracy under the Kaiser had been very limited. Article 48 of the Constitution allowed the President to announce a 'state of emergency', and bypass the Reichstag by ruling by decree)

• the Treaty of Versailles (terms, and attitudes in Germany; dictated peace or **Diktat**; War Guilt clause; the 'November Criminals')

• opposition to the Weimar Republic (pro-Kaiser officials; Communist rebellion in Bavaria; Kapp's **Putsch** [armed revolt]; Red Rising in the Ruhr; the Beer Hall Putsch)

• economic and social problems (hardship of early 1920s; French invasion of the Ruhr; hyper-inflation of 1923)

• the Stresemann Years, 1924-29 (diplomatic successes, economic and social improvement; liberalism in the arts; the flourishing of the arts in Weimar Germany, especially architecture – the Bauhaus – and the cinema; the replacement of France by Germany as the cultural centre of Europe – the period 1924-29 became known as the 'Golden Twenties')

This section deals with Weimar Germany 1919-29, before the Great Depression, focusing on:

■ the Weimar Constitution

■ the Stresemann Years 1924-29

This section tests your skills of comprehension and inference, i.e. understanding historical sources, and explaining what you can learn from them.

You need to learn these key facts:

The Weimar Constitution

■ The new constitution was Germany's first experience of a real democracy. Before 1919, the **Kaiser** (emperor) controlled the government, foreign affairs and the armed forces.

■ Weimar set up a new **Reichstag** (parliament) elected by everybody over twenty in a secret ballot, every four years.

■ Seats in the Reichstag were awarded by proportional representation (PR), so that if a party won 35% of the votes for example, it got 35% of the seats.

■ The constitution included Fundamental Rights (individual citizens' rights).

■ Weimar set up a federal system in which power was shared between the central government in Berlin and 18 new **Länder** (state) governments.

■ A president was elected separately, for seven years, to act as a check on the Reichstag's power.

■ But there were potential problems: although the Kaiser had fled, the senior civil servants, judges, police chiefs and army officers who had supported him kept their jobs. In addition, in the four difficult years 1919-23, Germany had nine coalition governments.

The Stresemann Years, 1924-29

1923   In September, Gustav Stresemann became **Chancellor** (prime minister) and took immediate steps to end hyper-inflation and the French occupation of the Ruhr. He stopped passive resistance to the French, and promised to pay reparations – the French and Belgians then left. In November, he introduced a new currency (the Rentenmark) to end inflation, and negotiated US loans to re-start the economy.

1924   Economic stability returned – Stresemann became Foreign Minister (until his death in 1929). His main aims were to 'revise' parts of the Versailles Treaty and to get Germany accepted as an equal in Europe. He also negotiated the Dawes Plan, which reduced reparation payments and arranged for loans to Germany from US banks.

1925   Germany signed the Treaty of Locarno, accepting the Western borders agreed at Versailles. This reduced tension with France.

1926   Germany was allowed to join the League of Nations.

1928   Germany signed the Kellogg-Briand Pact, renouncing war as a way of resolving disputes between countries.

1929   The Young Plan reduced reparations again, and extended the repayment period. By then, Germany's industry had recovered and exports were expanding.

The Weimar Constitution

Here is a source showing the results of the elections in Germany 1919-28.

	% of votes won				
	1919	**1920**	**1924**		**1928**
			May	*Dec*	
German Communist Party (KPD)	-	2	12	9	11
Social Democratic Party (SPD)	38	21	21	26	30
German Democratic Party (DDP)	19	8	6	6	5
Centre Party	20	18	17	18	15
German People's Party (DVP)	4	14	9	10	9
German Nationalist Party (DNVP)	10	15	19	21	14
Nazi Party (NSDAP)	-	-	7	3	2
Other (minor) parties	9	22	9	7	14

 REMEMBER Comprehension questions ask you to show that you understand the information in a source. Sometimes, you will need to point out two or three separate pieces of information.

 According to this source, which three parties tended to dominate the elections of this period?

 What do these election results tell us about politics in Weimar Germany?

According to the source, the SPD, Centre Party and the DNVP dominated the elections.

Proportional representation meant it was difficult for one party to have an outright majority. Consequently, there were frequent coalition governments. Constant changes made it difficult to deal with the serious political and economic problems during the period 1919-23.

 REMEMBER To get high marks, it is not enough to list the main individual points from the source. You must also make your own overall inference from, or summary of, what the source is showing. Don't just copy bits from the source(s).

 *Highlight the three dominant parties and their percentage of the vote in the source.*

📺 The Stresemann Years, 1924–29

Study the source below, which is an extract about Stresemann's achievements from a history book published in Britain in 1979.

> Gustav Stresemann contributed greatly to the stabilisation of the Weimar Republic. He was working for the speedy withdrawal of all foreign troops from German soil, for the removal of the moral shame of the war-guilt clause and for Germany's entry into the League of Nations.
>
> By 1930, Germany was once again one of the world's great industrial nations. Her spectacular recovery was made possible by a huge amount of American investment; between 1924 and 1929, 25,000 million marks poured into Germany. By 1929 iron and steel, coal, chemicals and electrical products had all matched or beaten the 1913 production figures.

◎ *Highlight the successes mentioned by the source.*

❓ *Consider how you can use your own knowledge of the Stresemann Years to add to the information given in the source.*

 REMEMBER Identify the main successes separately. Make an inference, or write a summary, at the beginning or end of your answer.

Germany 1919–45

Practice questions – the Stresemann Years, 1924–29

Use the source above to answer the following questions. Allow yourself 20 minutes.

- According to the source above, what were Stresemann's main achievements?

- What can you learn from the source about potential weaknesses in Germany's recovery under Stresemann?

To be able to answer questions on this topic, you will need to know something about the following:

• the origins and appèal of National Socialism (Germany's defeat, the Treaty of Versailles, political and economic problems of Weimar Germany)

• Hitler, and his role in the formation of the Nazi Party (army spy, take-over of German Workers Party, formation of SA)

• the Munich Beer Hall Putsch, 1923 (including Hitler's trial and imprisonment)

• Nazi beliefs (*Mein Kampf*, the Party Programme)

• the Nazi Party in the 1920s (the 'Lean Years', or Years of Waiting; party re-organisation).

This section deals with the Nazi Party in the years 1920-28, focusing on:

■ the Munich Beer Hall Putsch, 1923

■ party developments in the 1920s

This section gives you practice at answering questions which require you to comprehend and use sources, *and* recall your own knowledge, to explain or describe an event or development.

You need to learn these key facts:

The Beer Hall Putsch, 1923

Dec 1922   The German government suspended reparation payments.

Jan 1923   French and Belgian troops occupied the Ruhr to take goods from Germany.

German workers called a general strike and Cuno, the German Chancellor, ordered 'passive resistance'.

Sept 1923   Hyper-inflation and economic collapse caused great suffering. Stresemann became Chancellor, ended passive resistance and promised to pay reparations.

Oct 1923   Hitler decided it was time to overthrow the German government. The Nazi March on Berlin (similar to Mussolini's March on Rome the previous year) was to start in Munich, Bavaria. The Nazis formed a *Kampfbund* with other groups against the Weimar Republic. This was supported by von Kahr, minister of security in Bavaria.

8 Nov 1923   After Stresemann took action against left-wing governments in Saxony and Thuringia, Kahr withdrew his support. However, Hitler decided to take over a political meeting in the Burgerbraukeller to force Kahr, along with von Lossow and von Seisser (in charge, respectively, of the Bavarian army and police), to support the march.

9 Nov 1923   Supported by Ludendorff (a commander in the First World War), the Nazis' SA took over the army HQ in Bavaria. However, Kahr and Lossow changed their minds, so Hitler organised a mass demonstration. The police opened fire: sixteen Nazis were killed and Hitler fled. He and Ludendorff were later arrested, and put on trial for high treason. Hitler was allowed to make long speeches at his trial – the sympathetic judges acquitted Ludendorff, and gave Hitler a five-year sentence. After nine months in Landsberg Prison, Hitler was released.

The Nazi Party in the 1920s

1924   Trial and imprisonment of Hitler for high treason after the Beer Hall Putsch. Hitler wrote *Mein Kampf* (*My Struggle*) in Landsberg Prison. He was released after serving nine months of a five-year sentence. The Nazis did badly in the December 1924 elections (won fourteen seats).

1925   The Nazi Party was refounded after it had split and been banned. The SA (**Sturmabteilung** – Stormtroopers), which had been set up in 1921, adopted the brown shirt as uniform, and the swastika became the official party emblem.

The SS (**Schutzstaffeln** – protection squads) were set up with the black shirt as their uniform. More radical policies were abandoned, e.g. the confiscation of firms was altered to apply only to Jews.

1926   Special organisations were set up to recruit students, teachers and young people.

1927   The party organisation was centralised under Hitler's control.

1928   Membership rose to 100 000, but there was another poor performance in the 1928 elections (twelve seats). The German economy experienced a fourth consecutive good year.

Germany 1919–45

The Beer Hall Putsch, 1923

Study these two sources, which refer to the Beer Hall Putsch of 1923, and then answer the question which follows.

A The government of the November Criminals and the Reich President are declared removed. The National Revolution has begun. This hall is occupied by 600 heavily armed men. No one may leave. A provisional government will be formed this very day, here in Munich. The army and police barracks have been occupied, troops and police are marching on the city under the swastika. Now I am going to carry out the vow I made five years ago when I was a blind cripple in the army hospital.

Source A From Hitler's speech at the Burgerbraukeller, 8 November 1923.

Source B Nazi Stormtroopers arresting the Mayor of Munich, 9 November 1923.

◎ *Using the two sources, and your own knowledge, explain what the sources tell us about the Beer Hall Putsch of 1923.*

◎ *Highlight the relevant points from the sources and/or from the details of their origins.*

Source A refers to the 'November Criminals' (and Hitler's injuries received in the First World War), therefore giving one reason for the Nazis' hatred of the Weimar Republic. It also implies the involvement of the Nazi Party's Stormtroopers ('600 heavily armed men' and 'the swastika').

Source B also shows the violent nature of the Putsch (men with weapons) and the role of the SA (two of the armed men are wearing swastika armbands), while the caption also refers to Nazi Stormtroopers.

From your own knowledge, you can add other causes (reparations, French invasion of the Ruhr, hyper-inflation) as well as referring to the events of 8-9 November (the Nazi take-over of the meeting in the Burgerbraukeller, attempts to force three Bavarian ministers to support them, the defeat of the Putsch, and Hitler's arrest, trial and imprisonment).

The Nazi Party in the 1920s

Study the two sources below, which refer to developments in the Nazi Party during the 1920s.

A

When I resume active work it will be necessary to pursue a new policy. Instead of working to achieve power by an armed coup, we will have to hold our noses and enter the Reichstag against the Catholic and Marxist members. If outvoting them takes longer than outshooting them, at least the result will be guaranteed by their own constitution. Any lawful process is slow. Sooner or later we will have a majority, and after that – Germany!

Source A An extract from a letter written by Hitler while still in prison in Landsberg Castle.

Source B A photograph of Hitler re-founding the Nazi Party in Munich, February 1925.

! **R E M E M B E R** Make sure you extract information from **both** sources and/or details of their origins. Then, do **not** forget to add relevant bits of your own knowledge.

◎ *Make sure you look carefully at your textbook and your notes before writing your answer to the practice question below.*

Germany 1919-45

Practice question – the Nazi Party in the 1920s

Use the two sources above, and your own knowledge, to answer the following question. Allow yourself 20 minutes.

■ Explain why Hitler altered the Nazi Party's organisation and political strategy in the years 1924-28.

To be able to answer questions on this topic, you will need to know something about the following:

- the impact of the Great Depression (US stock market crashed in 1929 [Wall Street Crash], resulting in the end of loans to Germany [Dawes Plan, Young Plan]. Germany saw a rapid increase in unemployment 1930-32 – over five million by 1932. As a result, political instability and extremism increased. Goebbels improved Nazi propaganda and organised mass rallies across Germany. Nazis began to get financial support from companies)

- the Nazis' rise to power (breakdown of the Weimar constitution with the failure of democracy in a succession of weak minority coalition governments [Bruning, Van Papen] ruling by decree; elections 1930-32; Nazis' emergence as a mass party; political deals; appointment of Hitler as Chancellor – only three other Nazis in the coalition government; new elections arranged for March 1933)

- the Nazis' destruction of the Weimar democracy (Reichstag Fire; take-over of **Länder** (German states); the Enabling Act; the banning of other parties)

- Night of the Long Knives (purge of SA; Hitler becomes the **Führer** (leader); removal of military opposition)

This section focuses on two aspects of the Nazi take-over of Germany, 1929-34:

■ how Hitler became **Chancellor** (the equivalent of prime minister) in 1933

■ why the Nazis were able to consolidate their power so quickly

This section gives you practice at answering analysis of causation questions. Such questions require you to examine a *range* of factors or causes connected to a key historical event or development. To get top marks, you need to do more than just list or describe a series of factors – you should try to evaluate the relative importance of each cause. Possibly, you might be able to say that one cause is more significant than the others.

You need to learn these key facts:

Hitler comes to power

1932 Hitler got 13 million votes compared to Hindenburg's 19 million in the 1932 presidential election. The Nazi Party greatly increased its vote and by July 1932, it was the largest single party in the Reichstag (230 seats).

Nov 1932 The Nazis won more seats (196) than any other party in election, but 34 fewer than in July 1932, while the Communist Party was still increasing its share (100 seats).

Dec 1932 Von Schleicher became Chancellor. He upset big business by proposing compromises with the trade unions. Von Papen proposed a deal with Hitler as Chancellor of a mainly conservative government.

Jan 1933 Political, economic and military elites finally persuaded Hindenburg to appoint Hitler as Chancellor of a coalition government dominated by von Papen and the Nationalists.

The rapid Nazi take-over

1933

30 Jan   Hitler appointed Chancellor.

27 Feb   A week before voting day, the Reichstag Fire took place. Van der Lubbe, a Dutch communist, was arrested at the scene.

28 Feb   The Reichstag Fire decree suspended all individual rights and banned the Communists from the elections.

5 March   In the elections, the Nazis won less than half the vote (43.9%) despite intimidation. Their coalition partners, the Nationalists, got 8% – this gave Hitler control of the Reichstag.

5-9 March Nazi Party Gauleiters (district leaders) took control of the Länder.

20 March   The first concentration camp was established at Dachau for political prisoners.

23 March   After SA intimidation, the Reichstag passed Hitler's Enabling Law, giving him the power to make laws for four years without consulting the Reichstag or the President.

2 May   Trade unions were dissolved.

23 June   The SPD were banned, and other parties soon disbanded themselves.

14 July   Hitler outlawed all political parties except the Nazis. Germany became a one-party state.

12 Nov   In new 'elections', the Nazis got 92.2% of the vote.

1934

30 June   Night of the Long Knives: Rohm, other SA leaders and some other political opponents, arrested and shot without trial by the SS.

2 August   Hindenburg died, and Hitler persuaded the army high command to back him as Führer - combining the posts of President, Chancellor and Commander of the armed forces.

📺 Hitler comes to power

Study the source below, which shows the results of the elections to the Reichstag, 1928-32.

Table of number of seats won by parties in elections in Germany, 1928-1932	1928	1930	1932 July	1932 Nov
Nazis	12	107	230	196
German Nationalist Party (DNVP)	73	41	37	52
German People's Party (DVP)	45	30	7	11
Centre Party	62	68	75	70
German Democratic Party (DDP)	25	20	4	2
Social Democratic Party (SPD)	153	143	133	121
Communists	54	77	89	100
Other	67	91	33	32
Total	491	577	608	584

⦿ REMEMBER For causation/analysis questions, make a rough plan. Don't just describe what happened, explain **why** it happened. Then summarise briefly in an opening or concluding paragraph.

⦿ REMEMBER Identify several different causes or factors. Show which you think are more important and which less so.

◎ *Why was Hitler able to become Chancellor on 30 January 1933?*

To answer this question, you need to look at Germany's economic and political situation just before the Great Depression and during the period 1929-33.

Try to focus on the relative importance or significance of the various factors, including:

■ the prosperity of 1924-28 which meant extremist parties such as the Nazis were unpopular

■ the impact of the Great Depression (withdrawal of US loans, banks collapse, huge unemployment, failure of Weimar government to deal with crisis, massive disillusionment)

■ the political weaknesses of the Weimar constitution (coalition governments, rule by decree, political intrigues amonge the elites)

■ growth of support for the Communists, but failure to co-operate with the Socialists, dating back to the events of 1918

■ the Nazi Party's growing appeal (ability to mount massive campaigns and rallies; Hitler as an orator)

The rapid Nazi take-over

Look at the source below, which shows Communists arrested by the SA in Berlin, shortly after Hitler had become Chancellor in 1933.

(?) *Consider the events of 1933-34 carefully, and try to identify several different factors, instead of dealing with only one.*

(?) *Think about how you can write a brief paragraph to sum up the cause(s) which, in your opinion, was/were the most important. This should help you avoid simply describing what happened.*

(◎) *Make sure you look carefully at your textbook and your notes before writing your answer.*

(!) REMEMBER First, work out a rough plan. Don't simply write down all you know about this topic. Focus on analysing and explaining **why** (not the details of **how**) the Nazis were able to establish their dictatorship so quickly.

Practice question – the rapid Nazi take-over

Write five or six brief paragraphs to answer this question, including a reference to the source above. Allow yourself 25 minutes.

■ Why were the Nazis able to consolidate their power so quickly?

To be able to answer questions on this topic, you will need to know something about the following:

• the suppression of trade unions and all other political parties (Ley and the Nazi Labour Front)

• the control of churches (Concordat with Catholic Church; National Reich Church; the Jehovah's Witnesses refused to serve in the army and therefore many were imprisoned)

• the establishment of a Nazi Police State (**Gestapo** – Secret State Police; SS terror; concentration camps; informers; control of police and law courts)

• propaganda, censorship and consent (Goebbels; mass rallies; cheap radios; control of newspapers, radio and cinema; consent – many Germans were pleased that Hitler's government took steps to end unemployment and to scrap parts of the hated Treaty of Versailles)

• indoctrination (control of education; youth movements)

• opposition and resistance to the Nazis (political parties; youth; churches; conservatives and the army – some original Nazi supporters began to have second thoughts towards the end of the 1930s. An army plot [the Beck-Goerdeler group] planned for 1938 was called off after the successful invasion of Czechoslovakia; some army officers tried to blow Hitler up in July 1944 – the Bomb Plot failed and 5000 of these July Plotters were executed)

This section deals with the consolidation of Nazi control 1934-45, focusing on:

■ the establishment of a Nazi police state

■ opposition and resistance to the Nazis

This section tests your ability to evaluate sources for usefulness. For questions like this, you need to focus on what information each source actually provides about a particular historical event *and* the nature of the source – who produced it, what its purpose was, what *type* of source is it, whether it is typical of the period. All this will help you decide on the accuracy and reliability of the information. However, make sure you write about *utility* – don't just turn it into a question about reliability.

You need to learn these key facts:

The establishment of a Nazi police state

Coercion and repression were important elements in securing and maintaining Nazi power and control. Particularly significant were the following:

The Gestapo   This was set up by Goring in 1933 – it was the Secret State Police (Geheime Staatspolizie) and its job was to discover the enemies of the Nazi state. It was allowed to use any methods, including 'Night and Fog' tactics (night arrests) and torture. The Malicious Practices Act, March 1933, outlawed all criticism of Hitler and the Nazi state. The Gestapo also used informers, and encouraged all 'loyal' Germans to denounce critics. Children were even encouraged to spy on their parents and teachers.

The SS   The SS (Shutz Staffel) had been sent up in 1925 as a personal bodyguard for Hitler. In 1929, Himmler took charge, and it grew from 200 to 50 000. After the Night of the Long Knives, it became independent of the SA; in 1936, all police forces, including the Gestapo, were amalgamated under Himmler's control. The actions and methods of both the SS and Gestapo helped instil fear in those thinking of resistance.

Concentration camps   Opponents of the Nazis, and those denounced, often ended up in special camps, run initially by the Gestapo. Soon a special branch of the SS, the Deaths Head Units, took them over. Conditions and food were poor, there was hard labour, and there was much brutality including fatal beatings and executions. Different categories of prisoners wore different coloured triangles of cloth e.g. red for political prisoners, green for criminals, pink for homosexuals. Between 1933 and 1939, over 500 000 Germans were held in prisons or concentration camps for political offences.

Opposition and resistance

Not all Germans supported the Nazis or were intimated by their brutal methods of repression. Opposition in particular came from:

Communists and Socialists   After they were banned and their leaders arrested, members of these parties set up underground organisations. They organised strikes, sabotaged factories and railway lines, produced illegal newspapers, pamphlets and leaflets, and painted anti-Nazi slogans. Many were caught and executed. Once Germany was at war, the Communist Red Orchestre group gave military secrets to the Russians. However, as before 1933, the Communists and Socialists rarely co-operated with each other.

Youth   Some young people resisted the Nazis from the beginning – many more did so after membership of the Hitler Youth movements became compulsory. Many were culturally opposed to the Nazis' – the Edelweiss Pirates, the Meuten, and the 'Swing Movement'. But there were also political resistance groups – the most famous being the White Rose group of students at Munich University. Their leaders, Hans and Sophie Scholl and Christoph Probst, were beheaded in 1944.

Churches   Many churchmen spoke out against the Nazis - for instance over their euthanasia policy towards those disabled or mentally ill, while some helped Jews. In 1937, 800 Protestant pastors were sent to concentration camps. The most famous were Martin Niemoller and Dietrich Bonhoffer (who was executed in 1945).

Examining sources for usefulness

The establishment of a Nazi police state

Study the two sources below, which are about concentration camps.

Source A A photograph of roll call at Oranienberg concentration camp, Berlin, taken in April 1933.

Source B Part of the regulations at Dachau concentration camp, near Munich.

The following are punishable with two weeks solitary confinement:

Anyone enclosing or hiding forbidden articles, or articles produced in the camp, in outgoing laundry bundles, or sewing them into pieces of laundry, etc...

The following offenders will be hanged. Anyone who does the following in the camp, at work, in the sleeping quarters, in the kitchens and workshops, toilets and places of rest: discusses politics, carries on controversial talks and meeting, forms cliques, loiters around with others; who for the purpose of supplying the propaganda of the opposition with atrocity stories, collects true or false information about the concentration camp... All punishments will be recorded on files.

! **REMEMBER** Make sure you comment on what both sources don't show as well as what they do. Discuss their nature, origin and purpose, to assess how accurate and/or reliable the information is likely to be. Here, you can use your own knowledge.

! **REMEMBER** This is a **utility** question, so don't start by examining reliability, or by commenting about whether it is a primary or secondary source.

◎ *How useful are these sources as historical evidence of what life in the concentration camps was like?*

Source A refers to the existence of a concentration camp. The uniforms of the guards and the prisoners standing to attention show life was probably strictly disciplined. However, it doesn't show any violence and the prisoners don't seem under-fed or physically harmed. Yet, it is only one point in time and therefore may not be typical. Also, it doesn't say who produced it – the Nazis, or an opponent.

Source B is evidence of the rules of a different concentration camp, and shows a harsh set-up. But, it doesn't refer to other punishments, and doesn't give any statistics to show if the punishments were carried out. Also, is it typical?

📺 Opposition and resistance

Study the two sources below, which are about resistance to the Nazis.

A

Erich Deibel: on 29 April 1940 he drew the symbol of the SPD – three arrows - on the wall of the lavatory in his factory, adding the words: 'Hail Freedom!' On 22 July the following year he chalked up: 'Workers! Help Russia! Strike! Up with the Communist Party!' and drew the red star and the hammer and sickle. He also listened to broadcasts from the BBC. Accused of sabotage and treason, he was executed on 15 August, 1942.

Source A An extract from a history book written in 1994

Source B A photograph of Hitler's meeting room, after the unsuccessful July Plot, 1944.

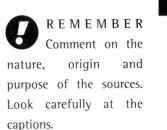

Germany 1919–45

❓ *Think about how the sources agree or differ, the positive and negative features of each source, and what they fail to show.*

◎ *Highlight any information given by the sources, and/or by the details of their origins.*

❗ REMEMBER Comment on the nature, origin and purpose of the sources. Look carefully at the captions.

Practice question - opposition and resistance

Study sources A and B and write two or three paragraphs to answer the following question. Allow yourself 15 minutes.

■ How useful are these sources for showing the extent of opposition to the Nazis inside Germany?

Life in Nazi Germany 1934-45

To be able to answer questions on this topic, you will need to know something about the following:

• economic policies (National Labour Service; public works; rearmament; conscription)

• Nazi propaganda

• Women and the 3 Ks (Children, Church and Cooking; employment and marriage laws; loans and medals)

• Jewish persecution (Nazi racism; Nuremberg Laws; Kristallnacht; Final Solution)

• young people in Nazi Germany (Hitler Youth)

• consent and support (degree and nature of support 1933-39; impact of the Second World War – shortages, bombing)

This section focuses on two aspects of life in Nazi Germany 1934-45

■ Nazi persecution of the Jews
■ Nazi policies for young people

This section tests your ability to deal with analysis and judgement questions. These require you to use your own knowledge to agree or disagree with a particular judgement of some historical event. You need to examine several different factors in addition to the one given in the quote, with your argument closely supported by carefully and precisely selected knowledge.

You need to learn these key facts:

Nazi persecution of Jews

Almost as soon as the Nazis came to power in 1933, they began to put their racist views into practice. Nazi racism was based on belief in the superiority of the 'Aryan' race, and was particularly anti-Semitic i.e. anti-Jewish.

In 1933, the Nazis had set up the Department of Racial Hygiene, the SA had organised a boycott of Jewish shops, and Jews were banned from all state jobs (civil service, the law, schools and universities, and the media). Worse was to follow:

1934 All Jewish shops were marked with a yellow star or the word 'Juden' (Jews). Separate seats were designated for Jews on buses, trains and in parks. Jewish children began to be victimised in schools.

1935 The Nuremberg Laws came into effect: Jews were no longer German citizens. This meant they had no rights and were not allowed to marry Aryans (non-Jews). Jews were 'encouraged' to leave Germany.

1938 After a Nazi official was shot by a Jew, there followed mass destruction by the SA of shops and synagogues in which about 1000 Jews were killed and many more arrested. This incident is known as Kristallnacht (Crystal Night or Night of Broken Glass). Jewish businesses were taken over, and Jews were forced to pay a fine of 1 billion marks.

1942 The Wannsee Conference took place at which the leading Nazis decided on the 'Final Solution to the Jewish Problem' and persecution turned into the Holocaust (1942-45).

Nazi policies for young people

All youth organisations were taken over. Young people were encouraged to join the Hitler-Jugend (Hitler Youth Movement, set up in 1925). This organisation was divided into five different groups as shown in the table below.

Age	Boys	Girls
6-10	Pimpfen (Little Fellows)	-
10-14	Jungvolk (Youth Folk)	Jungmadel (Young Girls)
14-18	Hitler-Jugend (Hitler Youth)	Deutscher Madel (German Girls)

Towards the end of the 1930s, membership became compulsory (although recent evidence suggests that not all children joined).

All members attended Hitler Youth camps every year. There were special schools for Hitler Youths who got the best marks: Adolf Hitler Schools and Order Castles.

The Nazis changed the national curriculum in schools in order to stress the achievements of Hitler and the Nazis and to blame any problems on the Jews, Communists and the Weimar Republic. Teachers who disagreed were sacked.

Nazi persecution of Jews

Look at the source below, which is a photograph of Jewish women and children being taken from their homes to an extermination camp.

 REMEMBER Be careful to answer exactly what the question asks – this question is concerned with **racial** discrimination and persecution, so you should **not** write about the various opposition groups (political, youth, religious) who also suffered during the Nazi era.

◎ *'Jewish people were the only group to suffer racial persecution at the hands of the Nazis.'*

Use the source above, and your own knowledge, to explain whether or not you agree with this statement.

❓ *Think carefully about your answer to questions like this. It is never advisable simply to agree with the statement. Such statements are based on the fact that there are always other factors, or sides, to be put.*

For this question, as well as selecting appropriate knowledge to show how the Jewish people were racially discriminated against and persecuted, you would also need to write about the treatment suffered by the Sinti and Roma (gypsies) and later by the Slavic peoples of eastern Europe.

⊡ Nazi policies for young people

Look at the source below, which is a Nazi poster urging young people to join the Hitler Youth. Then answer the practice question.

HER ZU UNS!

Hinein in die Hitler-Jugend

> **❗ REMEMBER**
> You need to do more than simply agree with the statement. The examiner has phrased the question to encourage you to discover ways you can disagree with the statement, or at least add to it.

❓ *Work out how you can give a balanced answer to the practice question. For example, show how some young people were either excluded from, or resisted, Nazi youth movements and propaganda, as well as writing about those who did become enthusiastic Nazis.*

Practice question – Nazi policies for young people

Write three or four paragraphs to answer the following question, making reference to the source above. Allow yourself 20 minutes.

■ 'Young people in Nazi Germany were enthusiastic members of the Hitler Youth movements.'

Do you agree? Explain your answer.

Here you will find answers to all the practice questions asked in this book. They are written in note form, but give the main points you should make in a good answer. In an examination, you would need to write full, grammatical sentences.

Medicine Through Time

p15

Source A shows **supernatural** beliefs ('evil things', 'gods', 'spells') about causes/cures of disease.

Inference: comment of 'successful many times' suggests that results were possibly recorded.

Source B gives **practical** advice for surgery, along with wrong ideas ('breath of life/death').
Inference: knowledge of anatomy probably gained from 'mummification', suggesting that there were also **natural** ideas in Ancient Egyptian medicine.

p19

Both sources are about dissection (humans in **Source A**; a pig in **Source B**).

From your own knowledge: dissection in Alexandria led to improved knowledge of human anatomy which Ancient Romans, such as Galen, tried to continue. But dissection of humans was forbidden in Ancient Rome (unlike Ancient Greece), so animals were used - this led to some mistaken ideas.

p23

For: the Church did control university medical departments and medical schools (via general control of education). The Church also taught that the Bible, Hippocrates and Galen provided all medical answers (even though translations of Galen's work were incomplete) and at first banned dissections, so preventing improved knowledge.

Against: by about 1300, the Church did allow some dissection and some minor changes to Galen's teachings. The Church also stressed care for the sick and began to set up hospitals (though for care rather than for treatment) in the later Middle Ages.

p27

Source A gives evidence of a new, more successful way of treating wounds (discovered by chance), while **Source B** shows Paré had experimented to find a better way to stop bleeding after amputations.

From your own knowledge: these ideas went against existing ideas. Though Paré published his findings (and had the support of the King), most doctors opposed him. Also, lack of antiseptics meant his use of thread made wounds more likely to go septic - while lack of anaesthetics meant long, complicated surgery was impossible.

p31

Main factors were:
Behring was able to build on the earlier work of **Pasteur** (germ theory, 1861) and **Koch** (the first to prove germs caused disease in humans, 1878), helped by **improved technology** (better microscopes, chemical dyes). Behring was also able to use a discovery by Pasteur's team (that germs produce **toxins**) to make his discovery of **anti-toxins**, enabling him to develop the first **cure** of a human disease.

p35

For: though it was a chance discovery, Fleming was the first person this century to show, by experiment, how penicillin cured infections without causing harm. During the Second World War, it was developed to become the most effective of all the 'magic bullets'.

Against: because chemistry techniques were inadequate before the Second World War, Fleming was unable to purify the 'mould juice' and did nothing more to develop it. It was Florey and Chain who made pure penicillin. Even then, it needed the involvement of large drug companies and governments (especially because of the war) to make penicillin widely available.

p39

For: both sources indicate that alternative medicine is successful (**Source A** says 81.5% recovered, while **Source B** indicates most alternative therapies rate 50-82% satisfaction).

Against: though used by many, neither source suggests alternative medicine is as effective as modern methods, e.g. we don't learn from **Source A** how many would have recovered using modern medicine.

p43
Source A shows a divided midwife - the male half using more scientific methods than the female half. But we don't know who produced it - it might be biased/untypical.

Source B shows male opposition to allowing women on to medical courses - again, this is only one example: other male students might not be so negative.

From your own knowledge: during the eighteenth century, obstetric forceps were widely used - the need for good anatomical knowledge to use them led to the gradual replacement of female midwives by men (at least for wealthy women). Also, there was great opposition to women studying for medical degrees in the 1860s and 1870s (e.g. the problems of Elizabeth Garrett and Sophia Jex-Blake); an Act allowing this was not passed until 1876.

p47
Source A shows how drinking water in towns could be polluted/contaminated, while **Source B** refers to lack of 'sewerage', 'drainage', 'cellar dwellings' and insufficient 'privies'.

From your own knowledge: during the Industrial Revolution, there was also overcrowding and poorly-built houses (e.g. 'back-to-back'), and poverty. These, added to those mentioned by the sources (sewage was often dumped in rivers used for drinking water), caused great problems, especially infectious diseases (e.g. TB, typhus, typhoid, cholera).

p51
Source A shows Archibald McIndoe performing a plastic surgery operation; he had been assistant to Harold Gillies.

Source B refers to emergency heart surgery on wounded soldiers.

From your own knowledge: McIndoe's work (aided especially by the use of penicillin), helped turn plastic surgery into an important 'high tech' specialism, so that today much can be done for those suffering from injuries/birth defects.

OR Harken's heart surgery (rare before the war) was so successful that it stimulated further research, therefore speeding up developments in open heart surgery, transplants, etc.

The American West 1840-95

p55
Source A shows closeness ('kinship') to nature and all creatures, while **Source B** gives an insight into beliefs about nature as a cycle which should be unbroken.

From your own knowledge: though we can learn something from these two sources, neither says anything about how Plains Indians believed spirits existed in animals, rocks, rivers etc. or about how nature should be respected, and how the land and its creatures should be passed on in good condition to the next generation (as land could not be bought/sold/fenced off).

p59
Main aspects of change were: by opening up the West, more settlers came and towns and ranches grew in size; the building of the railroads and the growth of towns increasingly disrupted buffalo hunting; railroads allowed wholesale massacre of the buffalo (for hides); as settlers increased, conflicts with Plains Indians became more common, leading to greater US army involvement.

p63
The **Source** shows one aspect of what was generally a hard life - collecting buffalo dung for fuel (trees were scarce on the Great Plains).

From your own knowledge: problems of housing (dug outs/sod houses), helping with farming jobs (including heavier tasks at busy times), as well as mother/housewife tasks (which were harder and longer because of lack of running water, etc.). Isolation was also a problem.

p67
Main reasons were: cattle which roamed over the open range often destroyed homesteaders' crops; there were frequent disputes over water rights/access to water; as permanent ranches were established, disputes broke out over land ownership/staked claims; cattle ranchers hated homesteaders' use of barbed wire, which destroyed the open

range; the collapse of the cattle industry in the 1880s saw cattle barons try to force homesteaders off the land - sometimes causing range wars.

p71
Source A is painted by a (white?) artist in 1899, twenty-three years after the Battle of the Little Bighorn. If the artist was present (we're not told he was), he might have forgotten or might have exaggerated the bravery of Custer and his men. It shows many warriors using rifles as well as traditional weapons.

Source B is painted by someone who fought in the battle, so he should know. However, his drawing does not emphasise Custer's role. Perhaps Kicking Bear was trying to belittle Custer? Also, seems to suggest that the Indians were outnumbered.

From your own knowledge:
Custer had divided his force into three groups. - those with him were defeated by a **larger** number of warriors, many of whom had modern repeating rifles. Overall, **Source A** seems more reliable.

Germany 1919-45

p75
According to the **Source**, Stresemann's main achievements were diplomatic (reversing parts of the Versailles Treaty, membership of the League of Nations), political ('stabilisation') and especially economic ('spectacular recovery', 'matched/beaten 1913 production figures' by 1929).

Weaknesses: recovery based on 'huge American investment' so therefore dependent on foreign investors/money market. Also, a debt crisis for German farmers and problems for heavy industry by late 1920s.

p79
Source A refers to 'armed coup' and 'a new policy'. Hitler was unable to carry out 'active work' because he was in prison (Landsberg Castle).

Source B shows that Hitler had to refound the Nazi Party in 1925.

From your own knowledge:
• new strategy necessary because of failure of Beer Hall Putsch, 1923, and Hitler's imprisonment
• while in prison, Nazi Party had split into factions and been banned
• prosperity of Stresemann's Germany meant a more peaceful route (winning elections) was necessary, including dropping the more radical policies (to gain backing of wealthy elites).

p83
Main factors were: conservative politicians misunderstood the Nazis' strengths, determination and intentions; opposition was divided, and failed at first to take Hitler seriously; Nazis used **legal** powers of Weimar Constitution to quickly consolidate power (e.g. Enabling Act); Nazis used violence to intimidate/crush opposition - both inside (e.g. SA) and outside (Communists, Socialists) the Nazi Party; political and economic elites co-operated.

Most important were swift use of legal powers and use of violence.

p87
Source A refers to examples of political/industrial opposition (slogans, attempts to organise strikes), but it doesn't show how common/widespread (i.e. typical) this was, e.g. no numbers given of those involved.

Source B shows an attempt to assassinate Hitler, but it doesn't say which individual/group was responsible and again, we are not told how common such attempts were.

From your own knowledge:
we know that Communists and Socialists did organise propaganda, sabotage, strikes etc. and that elements in the army opposed Hitler, but neither source mentions opposition from young people or members of churches.

p91
Agree: because of indoctrination in schools, and the more enjoyable aspects of Hitler Youth organisations (chance to miss school, weekend trips, summer camps, chance for girls to do activities not linked to wife/mother role), undoubtedly many children did support Nazis (some even reported on their parents).

Against: many young people disliked the Hitler Youth and the Nazis, either for cultural reasons (e.g. Edelweiss Pirates, Meuten and Swing Movement) or for political reasons (White Rose Group). In addition, young Jewish people did not become supporters - they were banned from youth organisations.

Glossary

Medicine Through Time

Anaesthetic a drug to make a patient unconscious, and therefore unaware of pain, during surgery

Antibody a defensive substance produced in the body to neutralise a foreign micro-organism or poison

Antibiotic a drug made from a living organism, such as fungi, which kills bacteria, or prevents it from growing

Antisepsis the use of antiseptics (first carbolic acid) to kill germs

Anti-toxin a substance, produced by the body to fight the poison/toxin introduced by a germ, which can be injected into another person to cure a disease

Apothecary someone (without formal medical training, at first) who sold drugs/medicine, usually from a shop.

Asclepion a healing temple in Ancient Greece (and Rome), dedicated to Asclepios, the god of healing

Asepsis sterilising the air, the clothing and doctors' tools in the operating room to remove the risk of germs

Barber-surgeons barbers who also performed minor surgery and dentistry. They were used mainly by the poor

Bleeding a treatment, based on the Ancient Greek theory of the Four Humours, to draw off an imbalance/excess of blood. Later called venesection

Cauterise a method of treating amputated limbs or wounds by burning them with hot iron (cautery) or oil to prevent infection and seal the wound

Clinical observation the close observation and recording of a patient's symptoms, followed by appropriate treatment, stressed by Hippocrates and his followers (in part, developed from Ancient Egyptian medicine). It is the basis of modern scientific medicine.

Embalming the practice of preserving a corpse from decay, sometimes called 'mummification', which was popular in Ancient Egypt

Inoculation an early method of protecting people from a disease, by infecting them with a milder form of the disease, in the hope of giving immunity (hence: immunisation)

Magic bullet a man-made chemical, designed to cure a disease by acting like an anti-body, without harming the rest of the patient's body

Natural something which is physical, observable and of this world

Pilgrimage a journey to a shrine or holy place

Plague there are two main types: bubonic (with buboes or lumps), spread by flea bites; and pneumonic (respiratory), spread by coughing or sneezing

Plastic surgery specialised surgery to repair badly damaged skin or birth defects

Quacks doctors who sold useless pills etc., often at fairs or markets, mostly to poor people - such medicine was known as 'quackery'

Regimen Ancient Greek belief that in order to be healthy, proper diet, sleep, exercise etc. were important

Renaissance rebirth; marked the transition from medieval to early modern history beginning in the fourteenth century; a period when the arts and sciences flourished

Thalidomide a drug, withdrawn in 1961 because it was found to cause malformation in the foetus if taken during pregnancy

The Four Humours Ancient Greek medical belief that the body was made up of four substances, or humours. Any imbalance caused illness, so treatments were designed to restore balance

Trepanning the cutting of a hole in a live person's skull – also known as trephining

Vaccination a safer and more effective method of immunisation, based on controlled vaccines to give immunity to specific germs

Wise women local women who gave medical advice and help – used mainly by poor people

The American West 1840-95

Buffalo chips dried buffalo dung used as fuel on the Great Plains, by both Native Americans and the early homesteaders

Cattle barons owners of large cattle ranches who formed powerful associations, and took over smaller ranches in the 1880s

Coolies derogative name applied to immigrant Chinese railway workers

Counting coup the practice of Native American warriors of rushing towards an enemy and touching him with a coup stick (a pole about 8-10ft long) – considered more honourable than killing

Dugouts early homesteader dwellings hollowed out of hillsides (many places lacked trees for log cabins)

Elders older male members of a Native American band or tribe, who were part of a council which made decisions. They were helped by soldier societies (e.g. the Dog Soldiers of the Cheyenne)

Federal territories areas of the West which were not yet full states of the USA - the federal (central) government appointed marshals and judges to help maintain law and order

Ghost Dance a dance taken up by the Sioux Nation in 1890 – associated with Wovoka who said the dance would bring back all dead warriors and buffalo, and make the whites disappear. It was ended by the Massacre at Wounded Knee, November 1890

Great Plains the huge, often barren, grasslands (prairies) west of the Mississippi - in 1840, the Plains Indians and about 60 million buffalo lived there (whites called it the 'Great American Desert')

Great Plains Massacre the deliberate extermination of the buffalo in the 1870s by organised hunting (for leather), encouraged by the government, who saw it as a way of forcing the Plains Indians on to reservations. By 1875, less that 1 million buffalo were left; by 1890, there were only about 250.

Great Spirit a name given by those Plains Indian Nations which believed in one supreme being/creator - other names included Father of Life, or Wakan Tanka (the Great God)

Homesteaders early pioneer settlers/farmers encouraged by US government acts and land grants in the 1860s to farm on the Great Plains - this began a large migration to the new Western Territories

Long Drive the journey made by cattle and cowboys from Texas to the cattle towns - it could last two months

Lynching the illegal hanging by unauthorised people (e.g. vigilante groups) of someone suspected of a serious crime

Manifest Destiny the belief by whites that they had a God-given right to rule the whole of the USA, including (after 1840) the Great Plains where the Native Americans lived

Medicine men Native Americans believed by their tribe to have magical and/or healing powers – those with mainly religious roles were known as shamans

Mountain men early fur trappers who also helped open up the West by working out new trails (routes) and acting as scouts for wagon trains of early pioneers

Nations the main groupings of Native Americans - each nation had its own language and culture, and was subdivided into tribes and bands

Native Americans all the Indians living in America before the arrival of the first white people - sometimes called (Red) Indians or American Indians

Nomadic a lifestyle based on hunting, requiring people to move frequently in order to follow the animals hunted (e.g. buffalo on the Great Plains)

Permanent Indian Frontier the 'border' along the Mississippi, first agreed in 1830 between the US government and Native Americans. All land west was promised to the Indians - but this and later agreements were frequently broken by US governments (e.g. the border moved further west to the 95th meridian).

Pioneers the very first white settlers to begin the move westwards

Range War a violent conflict between rich cattle barons and homesteaders, e.g. the Lincoln County War and the Johnson County War

Reservations areas of land (often poor) 'granted' by US governments to Native Americans - they were supposed to stay on them and whites were meant to stay out.

Rustlers gangs who stole cattle on the ranges and the Long Drives, e.g. Jayhawkers

Scalping cutting off the skin and hair on the top of the head of a dead enemy. Plains Indians believed it prevented them having to meet their enemy in the afterlife – it also brought prestige/honour to the warrior. It was also practised by some whites

Sod houses another early type of homesteader dwelling – better than dugouts, they were made out of timber and turf bricks, with roofs made of sod and grass. Though cool in summer and warm in winter, they were impossible to keep clean, and they were damp and attracted insects.

Trailblazers mountain men and fur trappers who surveyed/pioneered the first trails (routes) West, e.g. Oregon Trail, California Trail

Transcontinental the spreading of the USA across the county, to link the Eastern/Atlantic territories with the new

Western/Pacific territories, e.g. by transcontinental railroads

Twister raging high wind/tornado, common on the Great Plains

Vigilantes people who (often because of the lack of reliable law officers) formed vigilance committees, and punished suspected law breakers (e.g. by hanging/lynching)

Wagon trains groups of pioneers travelling West together in wagons (pulled by oxen, mules or horses), led by a pilot (captain)

Germany 1919-45

Anti-Semitism racism against semitic (especially Jewish) people

Aryan a white person of non-Jewish descent

Beer-Hall Putsch Hitler's failed attempt to seize power in 1923. Also known as the Munich Putsch or the National Revolution

Coalition a government made up of two or more parties

Concentration camps camps in Germany for the Nazis' political opponents - the camps' first victims were Communists and Social Democrats. Not to be confused with the later extermination/death camps in eastern Europe, set up by the Nazis for the Final Solution

Enabling Act the law pushed through after the Reichstag Fire which allowed Hitler to issue decrees without needing the Reichstag's approval - supposed to be an emergency measure for just four years

Final Solution Nazi policy to wipe out the Jewish race in Europe

Freikorps right-wing ex-First World War veterans (often unemployed) who formed armed gangs. Used to supress the Spartacist Revolution; many later joined the Nazi Stormtroopers

Führer means leader - used of Hitler especially after 1934 when he combined the roles of President, Chancellor and Commander-in-Chief of the armed forces

Gestapo the secret state police, first run by Goring, then, after 1936, by Himmler

Hitler Youth the various youth organisations (according to age and gender) set up by the Nazis to indoctrinate the young

Hyper-inflation vast increase in the cost of living due to the devaluation of the mark

July Plotters those involved with von Stauffenberg in the unsuccessful attempt (20 July 1944) to blow up Hitler

Kristallnacht Crystal Night, or Night of the Broken Glass, when thousands of Jewish businesses were destroyed

Länder the 18 local states/provinces of Weimar Germany

National Reich Church set up for Protestants by the Nazis in 1936, but many resisted

Night of the Long Knives purge of the SA (Brown Shirts) by Hitler

Nuremberg Laws the anti-Jewish laws of 1935

Passive resistance resistance/ opposition which tries to avoid violence, e.g. strikes, boycotts, non-cooperation. Used by Germans in 1923 after the French invasion of the Ruhr

Putsch sudden attempt to remove a government by force

Reichstag German parliament

Reparations compensation/indemnity payments - imposed on Germany after the First World War (£6 600 million)

SA Nazi Stormtroopers (Brown Shirts) led by Rohm

SS Schutz-Staffel (Black Shirts) – elite bodyguard for Hitler which, under Himmler, grew in size and importance. Used to purge the SA in 1934

Sinti a group of people who, along with the Roma, are often referred to as gypsies

Slavs people of Eastern Europe speaking the Slavic language – according to Nazi racism, Slavs (like Jews) were inferior

Spartacists members of the Spartacist League, led by Karl Leibnecht and Rosa Luxemburg who, in 1919, tried to start a Socialist Revolution. Crushed by the Freikorps, many of the survivors went on to form the German Communist Party (KPD)

The 3 Ks Kinder, Kirche, Kuche (Children, Church, Cooking) – the Nazi view of a woman's role

War Guilt Clause article 231 of the Treaty of Versailles – Germany was forced to admit total responsibility for causing the First World War and to promise to pay reparations (compensation)

Weimar Republic Germany's political system from 1918-33. Set up by the Weimar Constitution, it was Germany's first experience of real democracy